MW01122849

Our Lady's Message to Three
Shepherd Children and the World

Donna-Marie Cooper O'Boyle

Our Lady's Message

to Three Shepherd Children *and the* World

Illustrations by Ann Kissane Engelhart

SOPHIA INSTITUTE PRESS
Manchester, New Hampshire

Sophia Institute Press
Box 5284, Manchester, NH 03108
1-800-888-9344

www.SophiaInstitute.com

Sophia Institute Press® is a registered trademark of Sophia Institute.

Library of Congress Cataloging-in-Publication Data

Names: O'Boyle, Donna-Marie Cooper, author.
Title: Our Lady's message to three shepherd children and the world /
   Donna-Marie Cooper O'Boyle.
Description: Manchester, New Hampshire : Sophia Institute Press, 2017. |
   Includes bibliographical references and index.
Identifiers: LCCN 2017009900 | ISBN 9781622824564 (hardcover : alk.
paper)
Subjects: LCSH: Fatima, Our Lady of—Juvenile literature. | Mary, Blessed
   Virgin, Saint—Apparitions and miracles—Portugal—Fàtima—Juvenile
   literature.
Classification: LCC BT660.F3 O263 2017 | DDC 232.91/70946945—dc23
LC record available at https://lccn.loc.gov/2017009900

First printing

With great love to all of my children, Justin,
Chaldea, Jessica, Joseph, and Mary-Catherine,
and to my grandson, Shepherd James.
And to the Immaculate Heart of Mary, Our
Lady of Fatima, our Queen of Heaven and Earth,
who is the cause of our joy! May she be everywhere
blessed, today and always, on earth and in heaven!

Contents

Appendices

Note to Parents, Grandparents, Teachers, and Guardians

FROM FR. ANDREW APOSTOLI, C.F.R.

*O*ur Lady's Message to Three Shepherd Children and the World* is a special gift for the hundredth anniversary of the apparitions of Our Lady of Fatima and beyond. It is a treasure for children and is sure to help them experience Our Lady's message for two reasons. The first is that its author, Donna-Marie Cooper O'Boyle, is very dedicated to our Blessed Lady. No one can write with intensity and conviction who doesn't love the one they are writing about. Donna-Marie has a great love of Our Lady and has shown this in many of her previous books, shows, and writings.

The second reason this is a special gift for children and grandchildren is that Donna-Marie is a mother and a grandmother. Her understanding of children shines through in her loving descriptions of the Fatima events and as she encourages children to grow in holiness.

I highly recommend this book for children and grandchildren because it was as a child that I myself first heard about the message of Our Lady of Fatima. I saw one of the first movies about the Fatima events, and it left an impression on me all through my years of growing up. I never forgot it. Remember that little Jacinta, who was probably the most zealous of the visionaries, was only six years old when the Angel of Peace appeared to the children and only seven when Our Lady appeared to them. Surely the message made a profound impact on her. It has been said that if an idea is impressed on the mind and heart of children before the age of seven, they will never forget it. We need to bring our children to Mary at a tender age so that, as with Jacinta, our Blessed Mother's message may have a profound impact on them and guide them throughout their formative years.

Our Lady's Message to Three
Shepherd Children and the World

CHAPTER ONE

Three Shepherd Children

A long time ago—actually, about one hundred years ago at the writing of this book—in 1916, in a little hamlet called Aljustrel in Portugal, lived three cousins. Lucia dos Santos was the oldest cousin at nine years old, and her younger cousins Francisco and Jacinta Marto, a brother and sister, were eight and six years old. Lucia was the youngest of the seven children of Antonio dos Santos and Maria Rosa. Francisco and Jacinta were the two youngest of the nine children of Manuel Pedro "Ti" Marto and Olimpia de Jesus.

Though this threesome seemed like other peasant farm children of their age, something quite amazing would happen to them in 1916 and again the following year, when even more extraordinary miraculous events would take place in their lives. The supernatural events these three children witnessed would not only affect them profoundly but would also impact the entire world. That might seem too hard to believe. But, before we get into all of that excitement, let's first take a look at who the shepherd children were and what their typical daily lives looked like.

The three cousins were very close and were more like friends than simply family members. They were like you, in some ways, but just one hundred years ago, life was very different. Clothing was different from what you wear today, and electronic televisions, computers, and cell phones had not even been invented! Therefore, these Portuguese children lived much simpler lives than you do.

Lucia, Francisco, and Jacinta spent time together at each other's homes and would see each other at their parish, St. Anthony's, for Mass. But mostly, it was out in the fields and meadows that they were together when they were grazing their families' flocks of sheep. It was customary for the children of farming families to take care of the families' sheep. Even at their tender ages, the children were quite capable of herding the sheep out to the rolling pastures to graze during the day and to get them home safely before the sun had set and right on time to eat supper with their family. Can you imagine caring for an entire herd of sheep?

When Lucia grew up, she would later write in her *Memoirs* about the importance of the flocks and the responsibility of watching over them. She said:

As soon as the children reached the age of seven, they began to take their share in the running of the house by being taught how to look after the flocks. Like the Patriarchs and Kings of old, nearly every family had its little flock of gentle sheep which the children led out to graze in the green fields belonging to the parents. The flock helped considerably towards the maintenance of the family: milk and cheese, lambs to replace sheep that have grown old, or for sale on the market; wool which women of the house used to spin, dye, and then weave, in order to use later, to make warm colored shawls for the winter, or to make mats for the humble bedrooms, or round blue serge skirts with red stripes to adorn the Sunday clothes worn by the girls.[1]

THEIR FAMILIES

Francisco and Jacinta's parents, "Ti" Marto and Olimpia, raised their children in the Catholic Faith, as did Lucia's parents, Antonio and Maria Rosa. Their parents read Bible stories to them, taught them the catechism, and brought them to Mass on Sundays and holy days.

---

[1] Sister Lucia of Jesus and the Immaculate Heart, *"Calls" from the Message of Fatima*, trans. Sisters of Mosteiro de Santa Maria and Convento de N.S. do Bom Sucesso, Lisbon (n.p.: Coimbra Carmel and Fatima Shrine, 2001), 44.

Maria Rosa had a gift for teaching. Many times during Lent, after the evening meal, she would teach catechism lessons to young people who would come to the dos Santos house, often from long distances. These visitors were welcomed by Lucia's parents and would often spend the night.

When Lucia was much older she recalled that, even as a small child, she learned much from her mother's teachings. "My mother was a saint," she said.[2] She knew in her heart that her mother was a woman of great faith who was very humble and loving, always ready to help her own family and those outside it too. Lucia would later recall that she always listened intently as her mother taught her siblings, even though she was very young at the time. She explained about the lessons: "They were being absorbed into my spirit and stored in my memory, so much so that today I remember them with an intense longing for those happy times when innocence takes in

[2]   Fr. Robert J. Fox, *The Intimate Life of Sister Lucia* (Hanceville, AL: Fatima Family Apostolate), 65.

and stores up everything as happy memories for later times."[3]

Maria Rosa was not the only one to teach Lucia and her other children. Lucia's father, Antonio, also taught Lucia her prayers. He taught her how to bless herself with the Sign of the Cross; how to pray the Creed, the Our Father, the Hail Mary, and the Act of Contrition; the Ten Commandments; how to prepare for Confession; and more. This made Lucia's mother very happy.

THEIR FAMILIAR ROUTINE

Each morning the children dressed for the weather of the day, ate their simple bread-and-cheese breakfast, grabbed their long shepherd's sticks, which were used to help herd the sheep, and set out with their sheep to meet up with each other. They coaxed their flocks over pebbled trails and open fields to the favorite grazing spots, in areas called the Cabeco and the Cova da

[3] Ibid.

Iria. They had no idea at that time that truly wondrous heavenly events would occur there.

The three young shepherds had been grazing their sheep together for so long that they could hardly re-member when they began to do so. They were happy to tend their families' flocks together and felt very safe and content in their familiar routines.

Day after day, Lucia, Francisco, and Jacinta would try to find a shady spot close to some big rocks or under a tree and would sit on the soft grass to eat a modest picnic lunch of bread, fruit, and cheese that their mothers had prepared for them. Then they would pray a quick Rosary together and play imaginative games as their sheep pulled away at the blades of grass nearby. Many times Francisco would take out his little wooden flute and play a happy tune for the girls to dance to. It was a bright spot in their day.

Even though the children loved to play games and to dance and hop, they always kept a close eye on the sheep, or else their flocks might wander to another field for better-tasting grass. They might even get stuck in some brush or sharp brambles. It wouldn't be easy to untangle a scared, squealing sheep from the brambles, and the children certainly did not want their beloved sheep to get scratched or injured.

The threesome was familiar with the parable, or story, of the lost sheep, which we can find in the Bible. It says, "What man of you, having a hundred sheep, if he has lost one of them, does not leave the ninety-nine in the wilderness, and go after the one which is lost, until he finds it?" (Luke 15:4). The little shepherds knew how much Jesus loves His sheep and that He spoke to His disciples and followers about the Good Shepherd who takes care of his sheep—going after them and rescuing them if they are separated from the flock. The children's parents taught them that it was Jesus' love for every single person that made Him tell this story of the sheep. Jesus knew that God the Father does not want anyone to be lost—not even one sheep, or one person, as is told in the story.

After the shepherd finds his sheep that has roamed away from the flock and has been caught in brambles or maybe even on the edge of a cliff, he rescues it, and as the Bible says, "He lays it on his shoulders, rejoicing.

And when he comes home, he calls together his friends and his neighbors, saying to them, 'Rejoice with me'" (Luke 15:5–6).

This parable teaches us that we should care about everyone's salvation and should do all we can to help everyone — even sinners — to come to God. A shepherd rejoices when his lost sheep has been found and saved. Likewise heaven and earth rejoice when a person who has lost his way in sin finds his way back to God and is saved. The children would understand this parable even better after the wonderful miraculous events that would unfold, which we will talk about soon. The three young shepherds would learn to make sacrifices for sinners and realize why it was so important.

Back to the care of the sheep: Lucia, Francisco, and Jacinta did not want to lose any of their sheep! They loved them very much. Jacinta gave the sheep sweet names and sometimes would carry a small one on her shoulders to imitate Jesus. All three children were very good shepherds, who, even as they played, made sure that their families' sheep were safe.

Something to Think About

When Lucia was older, she recalled that, as a little girl, she used to listen carefully to her mother's teachings. She also had "happy memories" about her mother's lessons. Do you listen intently to your parents, your grandparents, and your teachers when they teach you about God? Do you think you will one day have happy memories about learning about your Faith? What can you do to learn more about your Faith each day?

CHAPTER TWO

A Surprise from Heaven: The Angel of Peace

There was a light, graceful breeze that morning, and the children thought it would be an ordinary spring day as they met at their usual place before taking their flocks to the fields. A few songbirds chirping their morning melodies occasionally interrupted the quiet that enveloped the countryside. The sky was bright and sunny as the three young shepherds walked up the beaten path on their way to the grazing spot. Something incredible was about to happen that the children would never have dreamed of—not even in a million years!

The cousins ate their lunch, said their prayers, and were about to play a game when the trees began to sway in a strong gust of wind. The children paused to look up. What they saw took their breath away!

A radiant angel, as white as snow, stood before them! He had the appearance of a fourteen- or fifteen-year-old boy.

"Do not be afraid. I am the Angel of Peace. Pray with me," he said to them.[4]

As astounded as they were, they felt at peace because the angel had told them not to be afraid. Lucia, Francisco, and Jacinta had learned about angels from their parents. They understood that angels are invisible helpers of mankind who behold the face of Jesus and praise and glorify Him. They knew that God sometimes

[4] Lucia dos Santos, *Fatima, in Lucia's Own Words: Sister Lucia's Memoirs*, ed. Louis Kondor, S.V.D., trans. Dominican Nuns of Perpetual Rosary (n.p.: Fatima Postulation Center, 1976), 62.

sends angels to earth. The Bible tells us that angels are "ministering spirits sent forth to serve" (Heb. 1:14). The cousins prayed to their guardian angels every day. But did they ever expect to see an angel in this life? No, they certainly did not!

Nevertheless, an angel now stood mysteriously before them. How could that be? They hardly had time to think about it. Heavenly graces enveloped them with peace, and they were comforted by the angel's greeting. They watched him intently and began to follow his example. They noticed right away that the angel was praying and that his posture was one of reverence. They watched the radiant being kneel and bow his head all the way down so that his forehead was flat against the ground. This was certainly a different way of praying. The children had never prayed with their heads touching the ground.

The angel had invited the children to pray with him, however, and they felt prodded by mysterious graces to kneel and to bow down to the ground. They didn't even ask one another before doing this—they all just did it at once.

Suddenly, the angel voiced a prayer: "My God, I believe, I adore, I hope, and I love You! I beg pardon for those who do not believe, do not adore, do not hope, and do not love You." The angel repeated this prayer three times. The children repeated the prayer. Then the angel got up and told the children, "Pray thus. The hearts of Jesus and Mary are attentive to the voice of your supplications." Then he vanished.

It was perhaps a little difficult to take it all in, but God's graces continued to fill the children's hearts while they were in the presence of the angel and after he left. They had never thought of themselves as being so special before this day. But now they knew that "the hearts of Jesus and Mary [were] attentive" to their prayers. Suddenly they deeply desired to please Jesus and Mary more than ever before and would continue to follow the angel's instructions to pray the prayer that he taught them. This prayer would become known as the Pardon Prayer.

Francisco had not been able to hear the angel speak, but he could see and imitate everything that the angel did as well as his sister's and cousin's gestures. Lucia and Jacinta could see and hear the Angel of Peace. The deep reverence that the children witnessed in the angel stayed with them. They chose to remain in a reverent position for some time after he had left. They stayed right where they were and prayed while the sheep grazed contentedly nearby. The young cousins felt a need to be very quiet and prayerful even into the next day. Their hearts were deeply touched by being with and praying with God's messenger.

THE MEANING OF
THE PARDON PRAYER

Why did the Angel of Peace come to the three young cousins that day when they were grazing their sheep? First of all, we can be sure that God had planned the special visit long before that time and that He knew for certain that the three children were innocent and possessed hearts open to His will in their lives. The Lord always chooses humble souls for His messengers.

Let's look at the prayer that the Angel of Peace taught the children. What do the words of the prayer mean? "My God, I believe, I adore, I hope, and I love You! I beg pardon for those who do not believe, do not adore, do not hope, and do not love You." This special kind of prayer is called an *intercessory prayer*. By sincerely praying it, we proclaim to God that we believe in Him, we adore Him, we hope in Him, and we love Him. We also tell Him that we know that not everyone thinks this way and that there are many who do not even believe in Him. Further, through this prayer, we ask that God would listen to our prayer and would please pardon the people who don't believe in Him. We can have every hope that when we sincerely pray this prayer, it will not only help our own souls but will aid others as well.

THE ANGEL COMES BACK!

A few months later, as the weather got hotter, the Angel of Peace surprised the children with a second visit. This time it was near the Santos family's home by a well. The children were playing their usual games, and suddenly the angel appeared right beside them. The children were a bit startled!

"What are you doing?" he wanted to know. But the angel did not wait for the children to answer. Instead, he immediately gave them a loving command.

"Pray! Pray very much! The hearts of Jesus and Mary have designs of mercy on you. Offer prayers and sacrifices constantly to the Most High."[5]

Can you imagine an angel telling you that you need to pray very much and that Jesus and Mary are expecting it, and that they "have designs of mercy" on you? The children were also told to offer sacrifices to the Most High God. That must have been a lot for them to take in. However, the children immediately felt up to the task. They wanted to please God and do the right thing. They didn't ask why they were chosen to do this important work. Instead, Lucia decided to ask how they were to make sacrifices constantly. The angel answered her:

[5] Ibid., 152.

Make of everything you can a sacrifice, and offer it to God as an act of reparation for the sins by which He is offended, and in supplication for the conversion of sinners. You will thus draw down peace upon your country. I am its Angel Guardian, the Angel of Portugal. Above all, accept and bear with submission, the suffering which the Lord will send you.[6]

This was yet another new way for the children to pray. When the angel came to them the first time, they learned the very reverent way of bowing down to the ground and the Pardon Prayer. On this second visit, they learned that they could and should make sacrifices for the conversion of sinners. The angel had explained to them that God was offended by sins, but that their prayers and sacrifices could greatly help. Amazingly, they were learning from the angel that their prayers and sacrifices could help convert sinners and even draw down

6   Ibid.

peace upon their country! They were also learning the value of offering their sufferings to God. The angel told them to "accept and bear with submission the suffering which the Lord [would] send" them. They were simple shepherd children, and God was entrusting them with such an important task!

The angel disappeared after telling them all of this.

The young shepherds now knew that their visitor was the guardian angel of Portugal. The girls told Francisco what the angel had said. All three cousins decided immediately that they would make greater efforts to say their prayers and would pray the Pardon Prayer more often so that God would be pleased. They would begin to offer sacrifices to please God and to help sinners.

A THIRD VISIT FROM THE ANGEL

The Angel of Peace made quite an impression on the children. They began to pray with much more fervor while out with their flocks, bowing down with their heads to the ground while praying the Pardon Prayer. They tried hard to offer up sacrifices to God as acts of reparation to make up for offenses against Him.

One day a few months after the second visit of the Angel of Peace, while the children were grazing their flocks at the Cabeco, a flash of light got their attention. Their heads had been bowed to the ground in prayer as their hungry sheep munched away at the savory grass nearby. All three cousins quickly picked up their heads to see what was happening. A bright light glowed all around them, and they soon discovered that the Angel of Peace was back.

Each visit from the angel brought more teaching and many more blessings. The young shepherds were being taught by an angel! Can you imagine that? These teachings and God's mysterious graces were preparing the children for what was to come the following year. We will get into that soon, but for now let us focus on the angel's third visit.

The Angel of Peace stood right next to the three cousins. He held a beautiful chalice in his left hand. A Eucharistic Host hovered above the chalice, and drops of Jesus' Precious Blood dripped from the Host and fell into the chalice. The children had never seen anything like this before. Lucia, Francisco, and Jacinta took it all in, feeling enveloped in God's abiding love.

What happened next was both mysterious and amazing. The angel left the Host and the chalice hovering in the air and knelt down next to the children. The Church teaches that we are not to adore angels. We should only adore God. We may pray to angels for help, but we don't worship them. In this visit, the angel demonstrated that he too was worshipping God as he knelt to pray with the children. In so doing, he had arranged a time of Adoration for them. They all put their foreheads to the ground in reverent prayer to Jesus in the Blessed Sacrament. The angel taught them another important prayer:

Most Holy Trinity, Father, Son, and Holy Spirit, I adore You profoundly, and I offer You the most Precious Body, Blood, Soul, and Divinity of Jesus Christ, present in all the tabernacles of the world, in reparation for the outrages, sacrileges, and indifference with which He Himself is offended. And through the infinite merits of His Most Sacred Heart, and the Immaculate Heart of Mary, I beg of you the conversion of poor sinners.[7]

The Angel of Peace directed the children to pray this prayer three times. He then got up and took the chalice and Host into his hands. He gave the Host to Lucia as Holy Communion and then said to Francisco and Jacinta, "Take and drink the Body and Blood of Jesus Christ, horribly outraged by ungrateful men. Repair their crimes and console your God."[8] It was the first time the younger two received Holy Communion—and it was given to them by an angel! The children had much to think about. The angel was teaching them about reverence and about Adoration of Jesus in the Blessed Sacrament. He told them that Jesus has been "horribly outraged by ungrateful men" and that they were being asked to "repair their crimes and console" God. That

[7] Ibid.,152.
[8] Ibid., 152, 154.

might seem like a very great task for little children. But we can certainly believe that God is very consoled by the innocence and reverence of children seeking to console Him. After all, it is Jesus who said, "Unless you turn and become like children, you will never enter the kingdom of heaven" (Matt. 18:3).

After giving the children Holy Communion, the angel bowed again and prayed the prayer along with the children three more times. He then disappeared from their sight. The three young shepherds stayed in their reverent, prayerful position with their heads bowed. They were enveloped in God's mysterious graces. After receiving Holy Communion from the Angel of Peace, they committed their lives to prayer and reparation. This meant that they would try their best to offer sacrifices and to repair, or make up, for the offenses of sinners.

Something to Think About

We have seen that the innocent shepherd children learned much from the Angel of Peace. We, too, can learn from him. We can try to be more reverent in our prayers. We don't necessarily have to bow our heads to the ground. But we can be more attentive and try our best to pray often for others and to offer sacrifices to God to make up for the times that He has been offended. We, too, can pray the Pardon Prayer:

> My God, I believe, I adore, I hope, and I love You! I beg pardon for those who do not believe, do not adore, do not hope, and do not love You.

We can also pray the second prayer that the Angel of Peace taught Lucia, Francisco, and Jacinta:

Most Holy Trinity, Father, Son, and Holy Spirit, I adore You profoundly, and I offer You the most Precious Body, Blood, Soul, and Divinity of Jesus Christ, present in all the tabernacles of the world, in reparation for the outrages, sacrileges, and indifference with which He Himself is offended. And through the infinite merits of His Most Sacred Heart, and the Immaculate Heart of Mary, I beg of you the conversion of poor sinners.

CHAPTER THREE

The Blessed Lady Appears

As far as we know, the children did not tell anyone about the visits from the Angel of Peace. They had wholeheartedly taken all of the angel's instructions to their hearts and continued to pray the special prayers when they were out in the fields and hills each day with their flocks. The children thoroughly enjoyed their days together playing and praying. Sometimes the girls would skip and dance in the sunshine to Francisco's flute, and other times, Jacinta would gather wildflowers and throw the petals into the air, as she had seen the girls do in Corpus Christi processions.

Being outside so often in God's beautiful creation gave Lucia, Francisco, and Jacinta much time to ponder His goodness in their lives and to pray—especially to offer reparation, as the angel had instructed them, for those who had offended God. The children worshipped God in St. Anthony's, their parish church, along with their families, but they also worshipped God in His "outdoor cathedral" in nature as they prayed each day. Their commitment to prayer can indeed inspire us all to praise and glorify God everywhere—not just in church.

On May 13, 1917, the young shepherds took their sheep to the grazing spot in the Cova da Iria (or Cove of Irene, which means "peace"). While the sheep happily nibbled at the grass, the cousins sat in a shady spot to eat their lunches. After rushing through a Rosary, they were just about to begin a game when the sky lit up with intensity as if by a huge bolt of lightning. Though there was no sound of thunder following the flash, the children quickly jumped into action to round up their sheep. They knew that it was dangerous to be out in an open field during a thunderstorm.

Another bright flash occurred, and suddenly a beautiful Lady all dressed in white appeared to the children. She was standing above a holm oak tree. Lucia would later say that the Lady appeared more radiant than the sun and radiated a beautiful crystal light. The children looked at her in awe. Before they could even think or wonder, the beautiful Lady put their minds at ease. She said, "Do not be afraid. I will do you no harm."[9] The oldest cousin, Lucia, knew in her heart that the heavenly Lady was not referring to any kind of fear that they might have had of her, because they were not afraid of her in the least. Lucia knew that the Lady was speaking of their initial fear of getting caught in a thunderstorm.

They observed her appearance as she stood before them on the tree. She seemed to be about seventeen years old. Her mantle and tunic seemed to be made out of light. A little ball of light hung from a cord around her neck, and near the bottom of her tunic was a star. The luminous holy Lady held resplendent rosary beads,

9   Ibid., 158.

and the crucifix on the rosary seemed to be illuminated to the greatest degree, giving off a dazzling glow.

THE BEAUTIFUL LADY
IS FROM HEAVEN

The cousins might have recalled that the Angel of Peace had put their minds at ease as well the prior year. He had also told them not to be afraid. Lucia immediately felt prompted to ask the beautiful Lady a question. She had a feeling that she already knew the answer, but she wanted to be certain.

"Where are you from?" Lucia asked.

"I am from heaven," the holy Lady answered.

Now that Lucia knew that the Lady was from heaven, she wanted to ask another question. Meanwhile, Francisco and Jacinta watched and listened attentively. Francisco could not hear the Lady.

"What do you want of me?" Lucia asked the Lady.

The Lady answered right away. "I have come to ask you to come here for six months in succession, on the thirteenth day, at this same hour. Later on, I will tell you who I am and what I want. Afterward, I will return here yet a seventh time."

Lucia, who always wanted to please God, decided to ask an important question that seemed to be burning on her heart.

"Shall I go to heaven too?"[10]

The Lady answered Lucia that she would indeed go to heaven one day. Lucia wanted to know about her younger cousins, Francisco and Jacinta, too. The holy Lady assured Lucia that they would also go to heaven, but that Francisco would need to pray many more Rosaries first.

The Lady had something to ask the children but was very patient as Lucia asked her more questions. She wanted to know where her two friends who had died were. The Lady explained that one was in heaven and one was in purgatory. Lucia and her cousins knew that purgatory is a place where souls who are waiting to get

[10] Ibid.

to heaven go. They had learned this in their catechism lessons. We, too, learn in the *Catechism of the Catholic Church*, "All who die in God's grace and friendship, but still imperfectly purified, are indeed assured of their eternal salvation; but after death they undergo purification, so as to achieve the holiness necessary to enter the joy of heaven" (no. 1030). Purgatory is a place for souls to wait while getting ready to see God. It is where they are purified so that they can finally be eternally joyful in heaven forever and ever. Purgatory is not a punishment as much as it is a gift of God's mercy.

A very good way to achieve holiness so that we can hope to go straight to heaven and possibly not need the purification of purgatory is through our everyday duties as Christians. Many of the saints have said that it is far better to work out our salvation while here on earth, by leading holy lives, following God's laws, and doing penance. If we sin, we should immediately seek forgiveness and make a good confession.

The saints have also said that the greatest suffering felt in purgatory is the longing for God. We know, however, that the souls in purgatory will be purified and will eventually see God in heaven. There will be much rejoicing when they reach heaven! We can all pray for the souls in purgatory and offer sacrifices for them so that they can get to heaven sooner.

THE HOLY LADY HAS A SPECIAL REQUEST

Lucia had finished asking the beautiful Lady the questions that were on her heart. Now the Lady would ask all three cousins if they would accept a holy mission from heaven. She asked, "Are you willing to offer yourselves to God and bear all the sufferings He wills to send you, as an act of reparation for the sins by which He is offended, and of supplication for the conversion of sinners?"[11] The children heartily agreed to do this. Of course, they could not see into the future. They did not know what kinds of sufferings God would send them. But they loved God

[11] Ibid.

37

and knew already that they could trust the holy Lady from heaven, so they did not hesitate to say yes. The Angel of Peace had helped to prepare their hearts for this holy mission when he had visited them.

The Lady then told Lucia, Francisco, and Jacinta that because they had accepted this immense mission, there would be much to suffer, but she also reassured them that God would see them through it all and that His grace would be their comfort.

Suddenly, a bright, glorious heavenly light shown on the children and all around them as the holy Lady opened her hands. Lucia would describe it later in this way:

> Our Lady opened both her hands for the first time, communicating to us a light so intense that, as it streamed from her hands, its rays penetrated our hearts and the innermost depths of our souls, making us see ourselves in God, Who was that light, more clearly than we see ourselves in the best of mirrors. Then, moved by an interior impulse that

was also communicated to us, we fell on our knees, repeating in our hearts: "O most Holy Trinity, I adore you! My God, my God, I love You in the most Blessed Sacrament!"[12]

Lucia, Francisco, and Jacinta continued to pray that beautiful prayer of adoration and remained kneeling in the transforming holy light from the Lady. They were at peace. The visit from the holy Lady would come to an end soon, but first she would ask something more of the children.

"Pray the Rosary every day to obtain peace in the world, and an end of the war," the Lady instructed. The children were more than happy to oblige her in this request.

But can you even imagine what the shepherd children were thinking after being entrusted with two great missions from the holy Lady in one day? They were asked to offer themselves to God and accept and bear all of

[12] Ibid.

the sufferings that He would give them "as an act of reparation for the sins by which He is offended, and of supplication for the conversion of sinners." On top of that, the Lady asked them to pray the Rosary every day to obtain peace in the world and even an end to war! World War I was raging at that time. Surely, at seven, nine, and ten years old, the cousins would not think of themselves as being capable of stopping a war. No. But the holy Lady from heaven said it, so it must be true. God's powerful graces illuminated the children's hearts and minds, preparing them for the great mission that was entrusted to them.

Then, as quickly as the holy Lady had appeared over the holm oak tree after the two flashes of holy light, she disappeared from the children's sight into the clear cerulean sky.

Can you imagine receiving such a special mission from a holy Lady who came down from heaven? The children were awestruck but completely at peace. They began to think about how they had previously rushed through their prayers and Rosaries every day, eager to play their games. They decided that they would pray more fervently and would no longer rush their prayers. After all, the holy Lady was counting on them!

PRAYING FOR THE CONVERSION OF SINNERS

After the visit from the beautiful Lady, the children remained very prayerful. The Lady hadn't requested secrecy, but Lucia sensed that it was best not to share about the miraculous visit from the Lady who came from heaven. Lucia asked her younger cousins to keep it a secret. Jacinta tried her best to keep it a secret but as soon as she saw her mother, Olimpia, later that day, she couldn't contain her excitement. She thought she would burst if she didn't tell her! She told her mother everything—blow by blow!

Olimpia thought that Jacinta must have imagined all of it. How could it be true? But, Jacinta's father, Ti Marto, thought about it all and decided that Jacinta was telling the truth. After all, Francisco wholeheartedly agreed with the story, and Ti Marto recalled that the Blessed Mother had appeared to other people in the past.

Not everyone believed that the story was true, however, and the children were mocked and made fun of. When Lucia's mother heard the news, she got very angry. Maria Rosa did not believe it could be true that a Lady came down from heaven, and she was extremely upset with her daughter for making up such a story that would embarrass the whole family.

It might not have occurred to the children right away, but the sufferings that the holy Lady had spoken about when she asked, "Are you willing to offer yourselves to God and bear all the sufferings He wills to send you, as an act of reparation for the sins by which He is offended, and of supplication for the conversion of sinners?" had already begun.

It was hard for all three of the children not to be believed and even to be ridiculed. Lucia especially felt awful to be scorned by her own mother and to be poked fun at by her siblings. Jacinta told Lucia that she was very sorry that she caused her such pain because she didn't keep the secret and had told about the Lady's visit. Lucia forgave her immediately. The children offered up their sufferings for the conversion of sinners.

Something to Think About

·————————————————·

In this chapter, we learned more about the children's prayer lives out in the fields, about purgatory as a place for purification, and about the holy Lady from heaven who visited the children and what she requested of them.

Can you consider praying to God more often and perhaps in more places? In addition, can you endeavor to pray your prayers with greater love and attention to please God?

Would you think about what you could do, in a sense, to fulfill your purgatory while on earth? Talk to your parents and grandparents about this. Together you can decide on some sacrifices and penances you can do.

CHAPTER FOUR

Another Heavenly Visit from the Lady

The three young shepherds carried out their daily routines but tried extra hard to pray their prayers more reverently and to make sacrifices to repair for offenses against God. They wanted to please God with all their hearts.

The Lady from heaven had promised to come back to see Lucia, Francisco, and Jacinta again. She had told the young shepherds to meet her at the same place "for six months in succession, on the thirteenth day, at this same hour." They were very excited to see her again.

But then Lucia started to wonder whether she should go back. So many people were making fun of her that she could hardly stand it anymore. Plus, her mother was convinced that the devil must be tricking Lucia. Poor Lucia was so worn down that she began to doubt everything.

Maria Rosa set up a meeting with their parish priest, Fr. Manuel Ferreira, hoping that he could tell Lucia that it was all a trick of the devil and that it was not a holy Lady from heaven. Fr. Ferreira listened carefully to everything Lucia said and concluded that she should continue to go to the Cova da Iria and see what would happen. He seemed to think Lucia was sincere but was not going to make a judgment just yet.

Though Lucia had been plagued with doubts about going back to the Cova because of all of the negativity and an interior turmoil she suffered, when the time came for the Lady to come back on June 13, as she promised, Lucia wanted to go back to the Cova with her young cousins.

THE LADY'S SECOND VISIT

On June 13, 1917, the three cousins woke up excited. They knew that this was the day when the heavenly Lady would be back, as she had promised. It was the feast of St. Anthony, the beloved patron saint of the Portuguese people, and the faithful parishioners enthusiastically looked forward to celebrating at Mass in the morning and then continuing to honor their patron saint throughout the day in the festivities that they called St. Anthony's *festa*. Maria Rosa was hoping against all hope that Lucia would not go to the Cova that day but would stay with the others at the celebrations.

With God's graces and the encouragement of her young cousins, Lucia had gotten over her doubts. She was more than ready to accompany Francisco and Jacinta to see the Lady. The children were still dressed in their church clothes as they made their way to the Cova after Mass, and some of the townsfolk followed them. Upon arriving, the young shepherds saw that many people were waiting near the holm oak tree for their arrival. Word had gotten around Fatima and the surrounding areas. The people had heard the story of the holy Lady who had appeared to the children the previous month. Many people had scoffed at the idea of a Lady from heaven visiting their little village, but many others chose to believe and traveled there to see for themselves.

Noon was approaching, and the three young visionaries knelt to pray the Rosary. The nearby people prayed with them. As they finished their prayers, the children saw a brilliant flash of light. Suddenly the light came closer to them, and the Lady appeared right over the holm oak tree again!

Lucia, as the oldest, took it upon herself to be the one to communicate with the Lady. She again wanted to ask the Lady what she had inquired the last time.

"What do you want of me?" Lucia asked.

"I wish you to come here on the thirteenth of next month, to pray the Rosary every day, and to learn to read. Later, I will tell you what I want," the Lady replied.

The Lady had told the children before that she wanted them to come back each month on the thirteenth and to pray the daily Rosary. But this was the first time she asked Lucia to learn to read. Lucia hadn't thought about learning to read prior to that day. She would do her very best to learn to read, however, because the Lady had requested it.

Lucia decided to ask the Lady if a person she knew would be cured. The Lady said that the person would be cured if he would be converted.

Something else was pulling at Lucia's heart, and she wanted to ask the Lady about it.

TALK ABOUT HEAVEN

Lucia knew that she and Jacinta and Francisco would go to heaven someday because the Lady told them so the first time she appeared to them. But Lucia had a burning desire in her heart to go to heaven now! She asked the Lady if she would take them to heaven.

The holy Lady responded in a way that Lucia was not expecting. She said, "Yes. I will take Jacinta and Francisco soon. But you are to stay here some time longer. Jesus wishes to make use of you to make me known and loved. He wants to establish in the world devotion to my Immaculate Heart."

Just for a quick moment, Lucia's heart sank. She didn't want to feel alone after her beloved cousins left this earth to go to heaven without her. They were so connected to one another through their Faith and their family, and now even more strongly through their heavenly mission.

She asked the Lady, "Am I to stay here alone?"

The Lady consoled Lucia with these words, "No, my daughter. Are you suffering a great deal? Don't lose heart. I will never forsake you. My Immaculate Heart will be your refuge and the way that will lead you to God."[13]

Lucia trusted the holy Lady. She had faith that the Lady's words were true and that God would help her with whatever she had to do — learning to read and staying longer on earth to help to make the Lady known.

Before leaving them, the Lady again opened her hands to radiate a mysterious holy light. The three children saw in front of her hands a heart that was encircled with

[13] Ibid., 161.

thorns that were piercing it. They instantly knew that it was Mary's Immaculate Heart that was seeking reparation for the sins that were committed against it. There was much grace in the heavenly light and the children were submerged in it. The holy Lady then disappeared into the sky.

God was working powerfully in the children's hearts.

Something to Think About

The holy Lady asked the children to pray the Rosary every day. Is this something that you could do, perhaps with your family? If you begin with even one decade of the Rosary each day, that would be a very good start.

At this point in the Fatima story, the children did not yet know for sure that this holy Lady was the Blessed Mother because she had not yet revealed that to them. But since this Lady from heaven was Mary, the Queen of Heaven, the children trusted her and followed what she told them. She said to Lucia, "Don't lose heart. I will never forsake you. My

Immaculate Heart will be your refuge and the way that will lead you to God."

Can you think of the Blessed Mother's words for a few minutes? Can you pray to her and ask her to help you to find refuge in her Immaculate Heart?

CHAPTER FIVE

The Three Secrets of Fatima Revealed

The Lady promised to come back on July 13, 1917. Word was getting around Fatima that the mysterious holy Lady was appearing to the shepherd children. Many faithful Catholics were hoping that it was the Blessed Mother who was coming to their village. Some just didn't know what to think. A good number of others still mocked the whole idea. So it was that a mishmash of people flocked to the Cova on that warm July day, wanting to see for themselves. About four thousand people showed up! This was abundantly more than were ever there in that once quiet field. The interest in the supernatural happenings was spreading like wildfire.

Every time the holy Lady came was important and exciting, but on this visit, she would give the young visionaries vital instructions about offering reparation to Jesus for offenses made against the Immaculate Heart of Mary. She would also reveal three momentous and amazing secrets. One of them was very scary.

The familiar flashes of light appeared, and suddenly the heavenly Lady was there, right over the holm oak tree, as usual. Lucia quickly spoke up to ask again what the Lady wanted of her.

"I want you to come here on the thirteenth of next month, to continue to pray the Rosary every day in honor of Our Lady of the Rosary, in order to obtain peace for the world and the end to the war, because only she can help you."

Lucia asked the Lady to tell them who she was and asked her to work a miracle so that everyone would believe.

The Lady replied, "Continue to come here every month. In October, I will tell you who I am and what I want, and I will perform a miracle for all to see and believe." She then added, "Sacrifice yourselves for sinners, and say many times, especially whenever you make some sacrifice: O Jesus, it is for love of You, for the conversion of sinners, and in reparation for the sins committed against the Immaculate Heart of Mary."[14]

The Lady had told them so much in this visit. She would reveal to them who she was in four months and would also work a miracle "for all to see and believe"! It was very exciting, but four months seemed such a long way away to the young visionaries. Waiting would be hard.

They now knew another important prayer, though. They would begin to pray it when they made sacrifices. We can pray that prayer too. We can commit it to memory and pray it as often as we can. "O Jesus, it is for love of You, for the conversion of sinners, and in reparation

---

[14] *Fatima, in Lucia's Own Words*, 162.

for the sins committed against the Immaculate Heart of Mary."[15]

But now something perhaps even more incredible was about to happen.

THE FIRST SECRET:
THE VISION OF HELL

As the Lady was finishing the prayer, she opened her hands again, and mysterious holy light radiated out. The light was not as it had been in the past. It seemed to open the earth! It revealed a very terrifying scene as the children were shown a vision of hell! It was only for a brief moment that they saw the fires of hell, the ugliest demons, and the poor charred and transparent burning souls of people suffering tremendously.

Lucia would later explain that she and her cousins were extremely thankful that the Lady had already

[15] Ibid.

promised that they would be going to heaven. Lucia said, "This vision lasted but an instant. How could we ever be grateful enough to our kind heavenly Mother, who had already prepared us by promising, in the first Apparition, to take us to heaven? Otherwise, I think we would have died of fear and terror."[16]

As devastating as it was for them to see this vision, the children now had absolutely no doubt about the reality of hell. This certainty and every horrifying detail they witnessed would help them greatly when they prayed for sinners. After seeing the vision, the little shepherds did not want anyone to have to go to hell! In fact, little Jacinta would often cry out, "Oh, hell! Hell! How sorry I am for the souls who go to hell! And the people down there, burning alive, like wood in the fire!"[17] Needless to say, Jacinta began to offer more sacrifices for sinners. She was a powerful little prayer warrior.

---

[16] Congregation for the Doctrine of the Faith (CDF), *The Message of Fatima.*

[17] *Fatima, in Lucia's Own Words*, 105.

THE SECOND SECRET: DEVOTION TO MARY'S IMMACULATE HEART

The children remained kneeling and looked up to the Lady in their sadness over having seen the vision of hell. The Lady said to them:

> You have seen hell where souls of poor sinners go. To save them, God wishes to establish in the world devotion to my Immaculate Heart. If what I say to you is done, many souls will be saved and there will be peace.
>
> The war is going to end; but if people do not cease in offending God, a worse one will break out during the pontificate of Pius XI. When you see a night illuminated by an unknown light, know that this is the great sign given you by God that he is about to punish the world for its crimes, by means of war, famine, and persecutions of the Church and of the Holy Father.[18]

[18] CDF, *The Message of Fatima.*

The young cousins took it all in. The heavenly Lady continued to tell them about many things, including another war that might start, terrible sufferings, and more. She said to prevent it:

> I shall come to ask for the consecration of Russia to my Immaculate Heart, and the Communion of Reparation on the First Saturdays. If my requests are heeded, Russia will be converted, and there will be peace; if not, she will spread errors throughout the world, causing wars and persecutions of the Church. The good will be martyred, the Holy Father will have much to suffer, various nations will be annihilated.[19]

The holy Lady told the children about scary things, but it was important for them to know and to learn how the bad things could be prevented—even the war could be prevented! Plus, their prayers and sacrifices could prevent people from going to hell. The Lady added a most

[19] Ibid.

hopeful message. She said, "In the end, my Immaculate Heart will triumph. The Holy Father will consecrate Russia to me, and she will be converted, and a period of peace will be granted to the world."[20]

The Lady taught the young visionaries a new prayer to pray at the end of each decade of the Rosary. It is known as the Fatima Decade Prayer. She said, "When you pray the Rosary, say after each mystery: O my Jesus, forgive us; save us from the fire of hell. Lead all souls to heaven, especially those in most need." You might have heard this prayer, or you might already pray it yourself when you pray the Rosary. The modern-day version is slightly different but holds the same meaning. It is: "O my Jesus, forgive us our sins; save us from the fires of hell. Lead all souls to heaven especially those in most need of Thy mercy." When we pray this prayer, we are asking Jesus to help everyone get to heaven, especially those most in need. This simple prayer underscores our duties to care for others and to pray for others. It is so

[20] Ibid.

important for us to understand the need to help others because our culture tells us to care only about ourselves and to do only what feels good to us. This mentality is contrary to God's way. We can pray that God will grant us the graces we need to be more loving to others.

THE THIRD SECRET IS REVEALED BUT KEPT SECRET

While the children were with the holy Lady, she revealed to them what is known as the Third Secret of Fatima. The young shepherds were instructed to keep this vision a secret. When Lucia grew up and was a nun, she wrote down the secret when the bishop of Leiria asked her to do so. The heavenly Lady had told her to do so as well. This is what Lucia wrote:

> At the left of Our Lady and a little above, we saw an Angel with a flaming sword in his left hand; flashing, it gave out flames that looked as though they would set the world on fire; but they died

out in contact with the splendor that Our Lady radiated towards him from her right hand: pointing to the earth with his right hand, the Angel cried out in a loud voice: "Penance, Penance, Penance!" And we saw in an immense light that is God: "something similar to how people appear in a mirror when they pass in front of it" a Bishop dressed in White "we had the impression that it was the Holy Father". Other Bishops, Priests, men and women Religious going up a steep mountain, at the top of which there was a big Cross of rough-hewn trunks as of a cork-tree with the bark; before reaching there the Holy Father passed through a big city half in ruins and half trembling with halting step, afflicted with pain and sorrow, he prayed for the souls of the corpses he met on his way; having reached the top of the mountain, on his knees at the foot of the big Cross he was killed by a group of soldiers who fired bullets and arrows at him, and in the same way there died one after another the other Bishops, Priests, men and women Religious, and various lay people of different ranks and positions. Beneath the two arms of the Cross there were two Angels each with a crystal aspersorium in his hand, in which they gathered up the blood of the Martyrs and with it sprinkled the souls that were making their way to God.[21]

It was quite a vivid vision, rich with meaning and symbolism. The young visionaries couldn't possibly understand its full meaning at that moment. However, the children realized and accepted that they must heed the message of "Penance, Penance, Penance," which the angel stated was essential.

The children learned a lot from the holy Lady in this visit. They committed their lives to taking on penances and making sacrifices to help save souls. They also offered prayers for the Holy Father. We, too, can pray to be more generous with our time and our prayers for others and for the Holy Father, our pope.

[21] Ibid.

Something to Think About

In this chapter there was talk about heaven and a terrible vision of hell. Three secrets of Fatima were revealed. There was a strange vision with an angel and a bishop dressed in white, soldiers, priests, and women religious. There were two more angels and a huge cross, and the blood of martyrs, and more. The holy Lady promised that her Immaculate Heart would triumph in the end. There is a lot to take in.

We can recall that the three shepherd children grew deeper in their faith as the Lady taught them important messages about the need for prayer and penance. She told them about the consecration of Russia to her Immaculate

Heart, and the Communion of Reparation on the First Saturdays. We will learn more about these things later.

For now, can you take a moment to think about your own life and how you might find more opportunities to pray and to offer sacrifices? You can pray at any time because prayer is raising your heart to God. It is taking time to have a conversation with God and pausing to listen to Him speak to your heart and soul.

Offering sacrifices to make up for sins against God can be done simply yet very sincerely. Think about ways in which you can make a sacrifice. One idea might be to give up something you like and ask God to use your little sacrifice of not eating a candy or a dessert to help someone in need. There are many kinds of sacrifices you can make. If you are sick, offer your sufferings to God and try not to complain. Do you remember the prayer the Lady taught the children and asked them to say when they made a sacrifice? "O Jesus, it is for love of You, for the conversion of sinners, and in reparation for the sins committed against the Immaculate Heart of Mary." Each time you make a sacrifice or an offering, you can say that prayer. It may seem simple, but its effects can be powerful when it is done lovingly and sincerely.

CHAPTER SIX

The Children Go to Jail, and the Lady's Visit Is Delayed

After the Lady had told the children such interesting and amazing things about coming back to perform a miracle in October and had revealed three great secrets, the children began to tell others about some of it. It was exciting, after all! But Lucia, Francisco, and Jacinta would not reveal the secrets because they knew they should not. Now people were more intrigued than

ever. Townspeople continually talked about these mysterious heavenly visits, and word about them spread to all
parts of Portugal. The newspapers, which were antireli-
gious for the most part, wrote articles about the strange
alleged appearances and labeled the believers "religious
fanatics." The reporters also criticized the local officials
for not having put a stop to it.

This angered a local chief official named Artur de
Oliveira Santos, who was very anti-Catholic. He did not
want to look foolish, and he therefore desired to prove
that the children were lying and finally put an end to
what he considered to be too much chaos and fanati-
cism for their little village. He arranged for the children
and their parents to visit him so he could question the
children about the "visits" and the "secrets."

Francisco and Jacinta's father, Ti Marto, went alone
because he did not want to subject his small children to
the long, nine-mile hike. Lucia went with her father. At
the Martos' house, before setting off on the journey, Lucia gave her younger cousins a hug good-bye. They burst
into tears thinking that Lucia might be put to death. The

impending interrogations were very unsettling for the two families, who wished that they could be left alone. Jacinta promised to pray hard with Francisco.

Administrator Santos badgered poor Lucia with one question after another, trying to force her to admit that everything about the heavenly Lady was a lie. He pressured Lucia to promise not to go back, but she wouldn't make that promise. He threatened to punish the parents civilly if they did not stop their children from going to the place where the apparitions took place. It was a grueling experience, but Lucia would not give in, and she, her father, and her uncle were finally dismissed from the administrator's office. Lucia stuck to her beliefs, no matter how much it pained her to go through such harassment.

August 13 was getting closer, and countless people were making their way toward the Cova da Iria. That once quiet area was bustling with activity from a multitude of pilgrims who wanted to get as close to the holy Lady as they could. Others who scoffed at the idea of the heavenly Lady wanted to get close too — so they could cause a ruckus and prove that the believers were wrong.

Administrator Santos was up to no good. He had conjured up a sneaky plan to stop the people from going to the apparition site. At least he thought it would stop them.

On the morning of August 13, the day that the holy Lady was to appear again to Lucia, Francisco, and Jacinta, Administrator Santos and a priest from a neighboring parish showed up unannounced at the children's homes. Santos told them that he wanted to go with the children to see the Lady because he wanted to be like St. Thomas and believe by seeing. His supposed change of heart was welcomed by the families, who wished to believe him. Santos offered to have the children driven to the apparition site in his buggy after a short meeting with the pastor. The three cousins went with Santos. Unfortunately, he had not told them the truth, and he had the buggy turned around and driven to his home instead of to the church.

After his wife served them lunch at his home, he took the children to the city hall to be questioned again. The questioning went on for hours, and since they were kept quite late, Lucia, Francisco, and Jacinta were then brought back to the Santos house to stay for the night.

Can you even imagine what went through the children's minds, being far away from home and with no way to let their parents know where they were?

Meanwhile, thousands of people had descended upon the Cova da Iria to see the Lady, or at least to be in her presence if they couldn't see her. The vast crowd stayed and prayed at the Cova even though the children were not there. They waited and prayed the Rosary. After a while, the crowds left the Cova quite disappointed. We can imagine that Lucia, Francisco, and Jacinta were extremely sad that they could not get to the Cova that day to see the Lady. They didn't want her to think they didn't care to go. But it was out of their hands because Administrator Santos had detained them. The Lady would know.

THE CHILDREN GO TO JAIL

The morning after the children were detained at the Santos home, Administrator Santos ordered that they be arrested. Imagine that! The young shepherds were all under the age of eleven. It's hard to believe that little children could be put in jail, yet they were placed in a cell with hardened criminals.

The children were saddened that their parents did not come for them. But because of all the confusion caused by Santos's devious plot, the parents were not even aware that the children were in jail.

The children decided they would offer up their fears, their sadness, and the pain of being in jail as a sacrifice to God to use for poor sinners and to make up for offenses against the Immaculate Heart of Mary. There was a time of mingling with the prisoners and encouraging them to kneel on the jail floor and pray the Rosary with them. That must have been a beautiful sight. It was certainly an image that the underhanded Santos did not expect to see.

One by one, the children were escorted out of the jail cell to be questioned again by Santos, who insisted that it was against the law to withhold information from him. Little Jacinta was the first to be snatched away and questioned. As intimidating as it was, Jacinta had a very strong will and would not give in and reveal the Lady's secrets. Santos got angry and told her that if she did not cooperate, she would be boiled in oil! She was escorted out of the room supposedly to go to her death!

Francisco was the next to be interrogated with endless questions. He also stood strong in his resolve not to reveal the Lady's secrets or to deny the Lady's visits. When Santos realized he wasn't getting the answers he wanted from Francisco either, he had him taken by the guard to the next room, where there was supposedly a cauldron of boiling oil. Lucia was the last to be questioned. She would not deny the Lady's visits or reveal her secrets. She told Santos that she preferred to die and go to heaven before revealing anything that she wasn't supposed to tell. She too was brought into the next room, where she was relieved with all her heart to see her two beloved cousins alive and well! The administrator had lied the whole time, trying to scare the answers out of the children.

Finally, on August 15, the Solemnity of the Assumption of the Blessed Virgin Mary into Heaven, Administrator

Santos let the children out of jail. He had them driven by horse and buggy and dropped off on the steps of St. Anthony's rectory when Mass was letting out. When the parishioners saw the children, they began to get agitated because they then realized that they had been abducted and thus kept away from the Cova a couple of days earlier. Ti Marto was there and calmed the people when it seemed that there would be rioting because of the fiasco with Santos.

THE LADY COMES BACK

On August 19, a bright Sunday morning, Lucia, Francisco, and his brother John brought the flocks of sheep out to graze at a place called Valinhos, just a short walk from their hamlet of Aljustrel. Jacinta stayed home that day. Lucia suddenly had a sense that the Lady might come. At around four o'clock in the afternoon, the familiar holy light began to flash. The children wondered if it was lightening at first and were ready to round up the flocks. Would the holy Lady come to this new place and without Jacinta present? Lucia asked John to run back home to get his sister. He said he didn't want to go all the way back. So Lucia gave him a couple of coins to coax him to get his sister. When Jacinta arrived there to meet the others in Valinhos, the Lady immediately appeared over a holm oak tree. It was the first time she appeared there.

This visit from the Lady wouldn't last long, but Lucia, again as the spokesperson for the group, asked the Lady what she wanted of her.

"I want you to continue going to the Cova da Iria on the thirteenth and to continue praying the Rosary every day. In the last month, I will perform a miracle so that all may believe," she told them. They were committed to praying the daily Rosary and were happy to hear from the Lady once again that she would perform a miracle. They couldn't help but think that the miracle would cause everyone finally to believe them.

Lucia asked the Lady about money that was being left at the Cova. The Lady told her that it was to be used for making "litters" to carry statues on the feast of Our Lady of the Rosary. Any other money would be used eventually to build a chapel. After she told them this, the Lady's face suddenly turned very sad. She said, "Pray, pray very much, and make sacrifices for sinners; for many souls go to hell because there are none to sacrifice themselves and to pray for them."

The children were deeply saddened to hear that many people go to hell because there are none to make sacrifices and pray for them. The young visionaries committed themselves to extra prayer to help sinners and to please the holy Lady. They took her words and sad countenance straight to their hearts and endeavored to make many more sacrifices. Francisco rarely played his flute anymore out in the meadows. The girls did not feel like dancing either. They decided that they needed to spend more time in prayerful reparation. They decided that they would make sacrifices too. For one such sacrifice, they wore thin ropes around their waists, under their clothing, and offered the discomfort to God.

Something to Think About

The children never expected that they would be arrested and put in jail. Yet, even though it was very hard for them, they did their best to do the right thing in a frightening situation by not revealing the secrets. They prayed and trusted God with the outcome. Can you take a few minutes to think about your own life and what struggles or difficulties you might be facing? Can you pray and trust God? Can you think about yourself in the position the children were in? What would you do?

With sadness on her face, the heavenly Lady told the children, "Pray, pray very much, and make sacrifices for sinners; for many souls go to hell, because there are none to sacrifice themselves and to pray for them." Can you try your best to pray more and to make sacrifices for sinners?

CHAPTER SEVEN

The Lady Appears Again

The news about the heavenly Lady had already been spreading around Portugal, but now people were also promulgating the latest scoop about the children being abducted. Indeed, there was quite a hubbub throughout the land, as well as masses of intrigued people who planned to make it their business to be present at the apparition site for the September 13 visit.

On that day, when the children began their hike to the Cova, the roads were all clogged. All that the cousins could see for miles around was an endless crowd of people walking toward the Cova! It was estimated that about twenty-five thousand people were coming to the Cova da Iria that day. The young shepherds had never seen that many people before in one place!

As the children continued on their way, people nearby began to recognize them and fell on their knees before them, begging the young visionaries to ask the Lady for a cure for them or for some answer to a prayer. The startled children were like little superstars. They certainly did not want that kind of attention, but the townspeople and people who had traveled from afar viewed the young visionaries as famous and very special because they had seen and communicated with a Lady from heaven. Seeing all of this commotion, and especially being at the center of it, overwhelmed Lucia, Francisco, and Jacinta!

They tried very hard to keep moving through the crush of people to make their way to where the Lady would appear. They didn't want to keep her waiting. It took some time, but the children finally made it to their regular spot by the holm oak tree. They knelt to pray the Rosary, and when they finished there was a flash of brilliant light and the holy Lady suddenly appeared above the tree once again.

Lucia again asked the Lady what she wanted of her. The Lady told her, "Continue to pray the Rosary in order to obtain an end of the war. In October our Lord will come, as well as Our Lady of Dolours [Sorrows] and Our Lady of Carmel. Saint Joseph will appear with the Child Jesus to bless the world. God is pleased with your sacrifices. He does not want you to sleep with the rope on, but wear it only during the daytime."

The children were so happy to hear that God was pleased with their sacrifices, and they would not wear the ropes any longer at night. Another sacrifice that the children made was to give all of their food away to any beggars they would see along the way to the fields. Little Jacinta was usually the first of the three to take their lunches to the needy, who often awaited along their path. Sometimes they fed their lunches to the sheep. Then, throughout the day in the fields, the children would eat a few wild berries or some fruit that might be growing on their parents' land. When hunger pangs summoned their attention, they offered their hunger as a sacrifice for sinners. The children would also go without drinking water for long periods, even in the blazing sun.

The children now understood that they didn't have to wear the ropes around their waists at night because God wanted them to get restful sleep, according to the holy Lady. Lucia, Francisco, and Jacinta would continue their daily Rosaries and had learned a while back not to rush through them. The Lady had said that Rosaries would help to end the war. According to the Lady, there would be much happening at the upcoming October visit. There would be not only a great miracle but also visions of Jesus, Mary, and Joseph!

Because so many people she had met on the way to the Cova had begged Lucia for answers to prayer from the Lady, Lucia felt weighed down with a huge responsibility to ask the holy Lady. She made it a point to ask her right away. The Lady told Lucia that she would indeed heal some of the people who had asked, but not all of them. And she reiterated that she would perform a great miracle when she came back in October so that all would believe.

The Lady then disappeared right into the blue sky.

Something to Think About

⸻ • ⸻

The three shepherd children were very determined to carry out the missions that were entrusted to them by the Lady from heaven. They made their sacrifices, prayed the Rosary every day, and were subjected to ridicule, as well as being thrust into the spotlight. This was not something the children were looking for. They simply wanted to be faithful to their promises to the Lady from heaven. But they offered these various sufferings lovingly to God.

Can you take a few moments to think about your life and what promises you can make to God, to Jesus, or to Mary? Are there sufferings or challenges that you can offer to God

lovingly without complaint? Can you be stead-
fast in your prayers each day? Can you pray for
all of the graces that you and your family need?
Always remember the poor sinners for whom
the Blessed Mother asks for prayers. Remember
that she said that many souls go to hell because
they have no one to pray for them. These are
some things to think about that can help you
grow closer to God.

CHAPTER EIGHT

The Great Miracle of the Dancing Sun

Lucia, Francisco, and Jacinta waited patiently for a whole month, anticipating the holy Lady's return. They made sacrifices and prayed many Rosaries, counting the days. The Lady had made huge promises, telling them that she would reveal who she was and perform a great miracle. The children were not the only ones waiting and yearning for the heavenly Lady and her miracle. Thousands upon thousands of people had also been waiting since September 13. Of course, there were still the naysayers who wanted to condemn the whole idea and had been growing weary of the entire hullabaloo. Lucia's mother, for one, was tired of people trampling down the family's crops on their way to the apparition site. Though Maria Rosa was a good woman, she often got angry with Lucia because of all of the commotion caused by the apparitions.

October 13 finally arrived. Pilgrims came from near and far to see the holy Lady and her miracle. They arrived by wagons and cars, and many came on foot, having walked or hiked a great many miles over a great many days to be there on the appointed day. The crowds had been steadily growing each month. Now, an estimated forty thousand to eighty thousand people were there in the Cova to see the great miracle the Lady promised. From as far away as twenty-five miles, approximately twenty thousand more people stood on hillsides to watch the happenings unfold.

A rainstorm had begun the day before, and the land was thoroughly soaked and full of endless mud by the morning. The rain seemed to be coming down in buckets, but the pilgrims trudging through the mud and the rain did not seem to mind their drenched clothes and the challenges they faced. They prayed as they traipsed through the storm and even sang songs along the way.

That morning, Maria Rosa excitedly told Lucia that they must get to Confession because if the Lady didn't perform her miracle, the disappointed people might become angry and kill them! Lucia knew in her heart that the Lady would come and would perform the miracle she had promised, but Lucia obeyed her mother and went with her to Confession. Lucia's father joined them. Maria Rosa also announced that she would go to the Cova that day. She said, "If my child is going to die, I want to die with her!"[22] So they made their way through the storm to the church for Confession and then straight to the Marto home to meet up with the family before heading to the Cova.

---

[22] John de Marchi, I.M.C., *Fatima: From the Beginning*, trans. I. M. Kingsbury (Fatima: Missoes Consolata Fatima, 2006), 128.

PEOPLE, PEOPLE EVERYWHERE

Lucia and her parents were surprised to see that a multitude of people had descended upon the Martos' home. People were coming in and out, and some cautioned them not to go to the Cova that day. They warned the young visionaries and their families that they might be killed by enraged nonbelievers. One woman they knew from a nearby hamlet showed up to bring pretty dresses for the girls to wear. When everyone was ready, the Marto and dos Santos families left the bedlam behind and set out together to see the Lady.

All along the way people kept calling out to the children, begging them to get help from the Lady. It was much more intense than the previous month. Though everyone was soaking wet from the pouring rain, they did not hesitate to drop to their knees in the mud to plead for help. The desperate people treated the children as if they were little saints who could work miracles for them, according to Ti Marto, Jacinta and Francisco's father, who would later tell about the dramatic scene.

The visionaries' families had a lot of trouble getting to the Cova. In addition to their being slowed by the blinding downpour and the people who were pleading for help, every inch of space was taken up by the pilgrims slowly making their way toward the apparition spot. At one point it was flat-out impossible to get through the walls of people. Ti Marto later shared, "The crowd was so thick that we could not pass through. A man who was a chauffeur picked up my Jacinta at this time and carried her into the field, shouting, 'Make way for the children who saw our Lady!'"[23]

The rush and crush of the crowd frightened Jacinta, who had never seen anything like this. The kind chauffeur put her down safely by the holm oak tree. She started to cry, feeling overwhelmed by all that was happening. Francisco and Lucia were on their way to join her. "They made it safely to the holm oak tree, but not before a man in the crowd tried to hit Ti Marto with a big stick. God's Providence through a protective group

[23] Ibid.

of pilgrims surrounded the assailant and prevented the attack."[24] Jacinta felt much better now that her brother and cousin Lucia were there with her at the holm oak tree.

"I AM THE LADY OF THE ROSARY"

The rain kept pounding down with a vengeance but Lucia felt a strong inspiration to tell the people to close their umbrellas and pray the Rosary. The holy flash of light appeared, and the Lady was there again over the holm oak tree. Lucia asked her usual question, "What do you want of me?" The Lady answered right away with exciting news about the horrible war and precise instructions as well as revealing who she was!

"I want to tell you that a chapel is to be built here in my honor. I am the Lady of the Rosary. Continue always

---

[24] Donna-Marie Cooper O'Boyle, *Our Lady of Fatima: 100 Years of Stories, Prayers, and Devotions* (Ann Arbor, MI: Servant Books, 2017), 83.

to pray the Rosary every day. The war is going to end, and the soldiers will soon return to their homes."

The children now knew that the holy Lady was "the Lady of the Rosary"! That meant that she was the Blessed Mother! How exciting it was to learn these facts, as well as that the war would end and the soldiers would come home to their families soon. The Lady of the Rosary also reminded the children to keep praying the Rosary every day and said that she wanted a chapel built there in her honor! The children couldn't begin to think of how they would accomplish that task, but they did not worry for one minute because they knew for certain that if the holy Lady said it, it would happen.

Lucia was feeling a bit weighed down by the pleas for help that she had encountered on her way to the Cova. So many people had ardently begged Lucia to ask the Lady for favors and cures. She needed to get it all off her chest, so she spoke up to tell the Blessed Mother that she had many questions for her about cures for certain people, the conversion of sinners, and more. The Blessed Mother in turn told Lucia that some would be cured but not all of them. She said that people needed to convert their hearts, ask for forgiveness, and amend their lives. She then said, "Do not offend the Lord our God anymore, because he is already so much offended."[25] This was a message that the Blessed Mother was directing to the entire world. The Blessed Virgin Mary knew keenly how the Lord suffered. After all, she is Jesus' holy Mother and suffers along with Him, as well as playing a big part in the redemption of the world.

THE GREAT MIRACLE OF THE SUN

As soon as the Blessed Mother gave that message to the children, she opened her hands and began to ascend. Lucia later described what happened in this way:

> Then, opening her hands, she made them reflect on the sun, and as she ascended, the reflection of her own light continued to be projected on the sun itself. Here ... is the reason why I

[25] *Fatima, in Lucia's Own Words*, 168.

cried out to the people to look at the sun. My aim was not to call their attention to the sun, because I was not even aware of their presence. I was moved to do so under the guidance of an interior impulse.[26]

While this miraculous light was occurring, the three young visionaries were completely focused on the Blessed Mother before them. They became unaware of everything around them—the weather and the noisy crowd of people. Heavenly light was pouring out of Mary's hands and projecting on the sun. The Blessed Mother was about to perform the great miracle she had promised.

The crowds of more than fifty thousand people had pressed in as close as possible to watch. Twenty-five thousand more were observing from the hillsides. The rain stopped abruptly, and the sun started to do crazy things. It grew much brighter and started to spin and

[26] Ibid., 170.

shoot out beams of light in every direction, causing everything to turn different colors. The sun then seemed to grow larger and larger in the sky and appeared as if it was being hurled to the earth! At this point, people felt sure that they were going to die. Almost everyone who was able to do so dropped to their knees and begged for forgiveness and mercy from God. The naysayers and scoffers were on their knees too. They suddenly found a reason to pray!

Then, miraculously, the sun went back into its proper place in the sky. The pilgrims' previously soaking-wet clothes were now as dry as a bone. The mud was gone completely, and the ground was dry. The sun shone brilliantly from a clear blue sky. The people were crying, "Miracle! Miracle!"

In his book *The World's First Love*, Archbishop Fulton Sheen spoke about the Blessed Mother's miracle at Fatima. He wrote:

At Fatima, the fact that Mary could take this great center and seat of atomic power and make it her plaything, the fact that she could swing the sun "like a trinket at her wrist," is proof that God has given her power over it, not for death, but for light and life and hope. As Scripture foretold: "And now, in heaven, a great portent appeared; a woman that wore the sun for her mantle" (Revelation 12:1).[27]

Can you even imagine seeing the sun spin out of control and hurl itself toward the earth? It was a frightening yet incredible sight to see, according to hundreds of recorded testimonies and eyewitness accounts that made it into the secular newspapers. Avelino de Almeida, a reporter for the popular newspaper *O Seculo*, made it his business to be present at the Cova da Iria that miraculous day. *O Seculo* had previously published articles that mocked the apparitions of Our Lady, but Almeida's story about the happenings of October 13, 1917, was different. Here is an excerpt from it:

[27] Fulton J. Sheen, *The World's First Love: Mary, Mother of God* (San Francisco: Ignatius Press, 1952), 273.

From the road, where the vehicles were parked and where hundreds of people who had not dared to brave the mud were congregated, one could see the immense multitude turn towards the sun, which appeared free from clouds and in its zenith. It looked like a plaque of dull silver, and it was possible to look at it without the least discomfort. It might have been an eclipse which was taking place. But at that moment a great shout went up, and one could hear the spectators nearest at hand shouting: "A miracle! A miracle!" ...

Before the astonished eyes of the crowd whose aspect was biblical as they stood bareheaded, eagerly searching the sky, the sun trembled, made sudden incredible movements outside all cosmic laws—the sun "danced" according to the typical expression of the people.... Standing on the step of an omnibus was an old man. With his face turned to the sun, he recited the Creed in a loud voice. I asked who he was; I saw him afterwards going up to those around him who still had their

hats on, and vehemently imploring them to un-
cover their heads before such an extraordinary
demonstration of the existence of God.... People
then began to ask each other what they had seen.
The great majority admitted to having seen the
trembling and the dancing of the sun; others
affirmed they saw the face of the Blessed Virgin;
others again, swore that the sun whirled on itself
like a giant wheel and that it lowered itself to the
earth as if to burn it in its rays. Some said they
saw it change colors successively.[28]

The Blessed Mother, Our Lady of the Rosary, had
indeed carried out the promises that she first made a
few months earlier, in July. The great miracle that Mary
performed was not simply for the benefit of the forty
thousand to one hundred thousand people (which includes the twenty thousand looking on from afar) who
witnessed it on that day. The great Miracle of the Sun

[28] Marchi, *Fatima: From the Beginning*, 137.

was for the whole world. It was a great sign from heaven, and it was to be passed down through generations and through centuries. You are learning about it now as you read this book. Future generations of relatives and friends will learn about it as well. This miracle and the Blessed Mother's message through her apparitions is timeless.

THE CHILDREN
SAW PRIVATE VISIONS

Earlier I mentioned that the children became unaware of what was going on around them when the Blessed Mother opened her hands and the brilliant holy light radiated out. That was when the miracle of the dancing sun began. At that time, the children were privy to their own miraculous visions. When Lucia was older she described it in this way in her *Memoirs*:

> After our Lady had disappeared into the immense distance of the firmament, we beheld St. Joseph with the Child Jesus and Our Lady robed in white

with the blue mantle, beside the sun. St. Joseph
and the Child Jesus appeared to bless the world,
for they traced the Sign of the Cross with their
hands. When a little later, this apparition disappeared, I saw Our Lord and Our Lady; it seemed
to me that it was our Lady of Dolours [Sorrows].
Our Lord appeared to bless the world in the same
manner as St. Joseph had done. This apparition
also vanished and I saw Our Lady once more, this
time resembling Our Lady of Carmel.[29]

These visions occurred in rapid succession. It was a
lot to take in, but the children were enveloped in heavenly graces. Their hearts and souls were totally immersed
in God and His blessings.

During these visions, the Blessed Mother was wear-
ing a blue mantle and was with St. Joseph and the Christ
Child, who were both robed in red. In all of her previous
visits to the children, when the Blessed Mother was over

---

[29] *Fatima, in Lucia's Own Words*, 170.

the holm oak tree, she wore white. In these private visions, St. Joseph imparted the Sign of the Cross above the people three times. When he seemed to fade away, Christ appeared at the base of the sun cloaked in red and with His Mother, who appeared as Our Lady of Sorrows but did not have the traditional sword through her heart. At that time, Christ gave blessings. When the vision ended, Lucia received her own private vision of Our Lady of Mount Carmel. Lucia's vision is noteworthy and meaningful because she would later become a Sister of Mount Carmel after first being a Dorothean Sister.

Can you imagine the astonishment of the countless people present at the Cova da Iria that day—both the devout and the doubting—as they observed the sun miraculously dancing in the sky? Those who had previously mocked the children were now believers!

Something to Think About

The Blessed Mother had indeed come through with Her promises. She revealed her true identity, worked an amazing miracle, and also asked that a chapel be built in her honor. People who were once unbelievers became believers when they witnessed the Great Miracle of the Sun.

The Lord God has sent His holy Mother to visit mankind at various times throughout history. He usually does this to wake us out of complacency and to ask us to pray (sometimes urgently) and to make reparation. The Blessed Mother at Fatima, also referred to as Our Lady of Fatima and Our Lady of the Rosary, asks us to pray the Rosary every day, to make sacrifices for sinners, and to make reparation for the sins committed against the Immaculate Heart of Mary. Her message was for the people of 1917, but it is also for us now and for those who will come after us.

We will discuss the offenses against the Immaculate Heart of Mary later on. For now, can you take a few minutes to reflect on what changes you might be able to make in your daily routine to try hard to live by the instructions that the Blessed Mother gave?

CHAPTER NINE

Francisco and Jacinta
Go Home to Heaven

U nless you ... become like children, you will never enter the kingdom of heaven" (Matt. 18:3). These are fundamental words from the Lord to ponder in our hearts. The three shepherd children had grown deeply in their faith since the first time the Angel of Peace had surprised them with a holy visit. They were already faithful and prayerful children, but God had a very special plan for them and thus prepared them for it. The three visits from the angel plus the six visits from the Blessed

Mother had immensely transformed Lucia's, Francisco's, and Jacinta's hearts, giving them a deeper understanding of the necessity of prayer and sacrifice. Not only would they get to heaven because of their lives of prayerful service, but through their prayers and loving sacrifices they would help others to get to heaven too. Though they were simple shepherd children, Lucia, Francisco, and Jacinta had learned to become selfless and had come to understand what was most important in life. They realized that life was all about preparing their hearts for their future in heaven and working hard to help others get there too. It was not all about seeking pleasure after pleasure. After seeing the sobering vision of hell, all three of the visionaries never wanted to waste any time or any opportunities to pray for poor sinners. They wholeheartedly remembered what the Blessed Mother said about the many souls that go to hell because they don't have anyone to pray for them.

Little Francisco would often take time to pray and quietly contemplate God and the instructions from the Blessed Mother on his own while out in the fields or at St.

Anthony's Church. He would often retreat to the quiet church when no one was there so that he could have some private time with the One he called the "Hidden Jesus"—meaning Jesus in the Blessed Sacrament reserved in the tabernacle. There with Jesus, Francisco surely received many graces and a deeper understanding of his Faith.

When asked by anyone what he wanted to be when he grew up, Francisco would always reply that he wanted to go to heaven. Once when talking to his little sister and to Lucia, Francisco expressed his joy over the apparitions and their meaning and how passionately he desired to please God. He said:

> I loved seeing the Angel, and I loved seeing Our Lady even better, but what I liked best of all was seeing Our Lord in that light which Our Lady put into our hearts. I love God so much, but He is so sad because of all the sins. We mustn't commit even the tiniest sin![30]

[30] Ibid., 172.

The time was drawing near when the two littlest cousins would be leaving their lives on earth to go to the glorious life in heaven that God had prepared for them, as the Lady had promised. Lucia would stay behind, grow up to learn more and more about her Faith, learn to read and write, and become a nun in two religious orders. Most importantly, she would spread the messages that the Blessed Mother had taught all three cousins. As we learned earlier, the Lady had told Lucia, "But you are to stay here some time longer. Jesus wishes to make use of you to make me known and loved. He wants to establish in the world devotion to my Immaculate Heart." We shall see just how long "some time longer" would turn out to be. But first, let us take a look at what happened a year or so after the great Miracle of the Sun.

"THERE'S WORK TO BE DONE!"

Before Francisco and Jacinta would leave behind their lives on earth to see God face-to-face in heaven, they had some additional work to do. Writing these words reminds me of my friend Servant of God Fr. John A. Hardon, S.J., who was a world-renowned theologian, very passionate about living his Faith and teaching others. He would often express with a twinkle in his eyes, "There's work to be done!" He meant that we must work tirelessly for the Kingdom of God. The importance of his message has stayed with me. He was such a hard worker in our Lord's vineyard that I am sure he was quite exhausted by the time he got to heaven. But that is a very good thing. His example can inspire us all to work hard for our Lord.

With regard to the messages of Fatima, Fr. Hardon said, "As you read the story of the original Fatima apparitions and the Church's explanation, you are struck by their utter simplicity. There are no subtleties, and no theological speculations." He continued with an essential question, "Three little children could understand—why? Because they had faith, they prayed, and they had a spiritual instinct for self-denial as a means of expiating sin." He went on to say that among those three, faith is the most fundamental, but it must be the true Roman Catholic Faith. He said, "That surely must be one reason why Our Lady chose such simple persons as the three children of Fatima, to share with them her concern over the sinfulness of mankind." What was so special about these three shepherd children who, according to Fr. Hardon, "were academically untrained, and in the eyes of a sophisticated world, three nobodies"? His answer was: "They had the faith."[31]

We should ask ourselves, "Do I have faith?" Faith is believing without seeing. The virtue of faith, which was gifted to us at our baptisms, should not grow stagnant in our hearts. It is like a muscle that should be used continuously. There is no limit to our growth in faith. Living a prayerful life of virtue and detaching ourselves from sin helps us to grow in our faith.

Pope Francis once gave a homily about this passage from the Letter to the Hebrews: "But exhort one another

---

[31] Fr. John A. Hardon, S.J., "Fatima and Miracles of Conversion," The Real Presence Association, http://www.therealpresence.org/.

every day, as long as it is called 'today,' that none of you may be hardened by the deceitfulness of sin" (3:13). Many times people put off praying or getting closer to the Lord. They'll wait for another day. They feel they are too busy, or they just don't want to put forth the effort. However, it is so important not to wait. We might only have today. We don't know the future. We need to seize every opportunity to grow in our faith and help others to do so as well. We must take the time and reflect on our faith "today."

Pope Francis said we should ask ourselves, "How is my 'today' in the presence of the Lord? And how is my heart? Is it open? Is it strong in faith? Is it led by the love of the Lord?"[32]

The children certainly had faith and worked very hard to offer sacrifices and prayers every day, especially as

---

[32] Junno Arocho Esteves, "Don't Procrastinate on Faith, Live Today, Pope Says," Catholic News Service, January 12, 2017, http://www.catholicnews.com/services/englishnews/2017/dont-procrastinate-on-faith-live-today-pope-says.cfm.

their days were coming quickly to a close. They wanted to be sure to do all that they could to help others get to heaven, where we are meant to live for all eternity in great joy with God the Father, His Son Jesus, the Holy Spirit, the Blessed Mother, and all of the saints and angels!

AN OUTBREAK OF INFLUENZA TAKES A TOLL

About a year after the great Miracle of the Sun occurred, a killer influenza epidemic spread throughout the land and even the whole world. It is said that twenty million lives were lost due to this devastating outbreak. The Marto family fell victim to it. It seemed as if God spared Ti Marto from becoming afflicted so that he could take care of his ailing family. Both Francisco and Jacinta became quite ill. They reminded one another to offer up their sufferings to make reparation for sinners and for the offenses committed against the Immaculate Heart of Mary. They also recalled the promises of the Blessed

Virgin Mary that she would come to get them soon and that Lucia would stay longer on earth to carry out the Lord's plan.

BRAVE LITTLE FRANCISCO

Francisco's illness got so bad that he could no longer be treated at home and was admitted to the hospital. Once, when he was in pain from a severe headache, Jacinta encouraged him to "make the offering for sinners." In almost a whisper, Francisco said, "Yes. But first I make it to console Our Lord and Our Lady, and then, afterwards, for sinners and the Holy Father."[33] Francisco was always mindful of making sacrifices and offering his sufferings to console our Lord and our Lady and to make reparation for sinners, and to pray for the Holy Father. He remembered well the lessons he had learned from so many heavenly visits.

During this time, Francisco would be blessed with yet another heavenly visit. The Blessed Mother appeared to

---

[33] *Fatima, in Lucia's Own Words*, 137.

him and Jacinta to tell them that she would be coming soon to take Francisco to heaven with her and then a little later on would come back for Jacinta. The Blessed Mother had given Jacinta a choice to go to heaven very soon or to stay on earth a while longer to save more souls. Brave little Jacinta chose to save more souls for heaven! The beautiful Lady warned Jacinta that she would suffer much in the hospital but that many souls would be saved.

Jacinta shared with Lucia what the Blessed Mother had told her and Francisco when she visited them. Lucia also visited Francisco in the hospital. It wouldn't be very long before Jacinta's illness would grow worse and she would require hospitalization too. Meanwhile, Francisco's fever rose, and he, his family, and his doctor felt certain that it wouldn't be long before this faithful young visionary would close his eyes to this world for the last time. Francisco requested Holy Communion. He had not yet officially received his First Holy Communion, but what could be better than to receive Holy Communion from an angel? The Angel of Peace had given

Francisco and Jacinta a drink of the Precious Blood from the chalice during his third visit. But now Francisco desired Holy Communion before he would meet his Lord in heaven. The priest who visited Francisco promised to come back in the morning to bring Holy Communion.

Francisco asked forgiveness of all his sins and shortcomings and offered up the pain and suffering of his illness for reparation and to console Jesus and Mary. He managed to get to sleep that night and looked forward to seeing the priest in the morning with his "Hidden Jesus." In the morning Francisco received his Lord in Holy Communion and closed his eyes in prayer afterward, savoring the heavenly graces. His family visited and had much trouble saying good-bye to sweet Francisco. They were consoled knowing that he would be extremely happy in heaven with Jesus, Mary, the saints, and the angels. They would see him again when it was their time to go to their own eternal reward of heaven.

On the morning of April 4, 1919, ten-year-old Francisco went to heaven. Just before he died, he called out to his mother from his hospital bed. "Mother, look at that lovely light by the door!"[34] The light was surely a sign from the Blessed Mother that she was there to take Francisco to heaven, as she had promised.

COURAGEOUS LITTLE JACINTA

The pain of not having Francisco near was almost too much for Jacinta's little heart to bear, so she kept reminding herself that he was now safely in heaven, enjoying the greatest joy ever. Sometimes tears would stream down Jacinta's face, and she cried to Lucia about how much she missed Francisco, who had been such a loyal companion in their heavenly mission to save souls. Jacinta felt sure that no one but Francisco and Lucia could truly understand her heart. However, Jacinta would absolutely keep her promise to the Blessed Mother to stay strong and offer everything to save souls.

This little visionary was also mindful of praying much for the Holy Father. She had received two private visions

[34] Marchi, *Fatima: From the Beginning*, 185.

of the Holy Father. In one vision he was weeping and there were many people outside his house, cursing and throwing stones. In the other vision, which she saw when out in the fields with her two cousins, the Holy Father was in church praying before the Immaculate Heart of Mary. Jacinta had recalled the words of the Blessed Mother when she appeared to the children for the third time, telling them of the persecution of the Holy Father.

Jacinta's illness grew worse, and she was taken to the hospital. She knew in her heart that there wasn't much that could be done to help her because the Blessed Lady had offered her the choice to stay longer in this world, and that meant that she would be suffering more intensely for sinners during the last days of her life. Yet this little girl was obedient to what needed to be done and that meant going to the hospital and offering her sufferings for heaven's purposes. Even though her body was weak with sickness, Jacinta's heart was on fire to save souls. She wanted to make up for sacrileges and outrages against the Immaculate Heart of Mary, as she learned from the Blessed Mother. This little prayer warrior did not want any souls to perish in hell. In addition to the pains and sufferings of her intense illness, Jacinta suffered from other pains too. It was sad for Jacinta that Francisco was no longer nearby and that Lucia could not visit her very often. But she remained courageous and stayed committed to her prayers and offerings, knowing and believing the Blessed Mother's promises to her during the two months she was at the first hospital.

Finally, when the doctors believed that nothing more could be done to help Jacinta, she was sent home to her family. She was still bedridden and feverish. She had a gaping wound in her chest. Even when she was suffering terribly, Jacinta always thought of others before herself. She had often encouraged Lucia to visit Francisco first before visiting her. She also told Lucia, "We must make many sacrifices and pray a lot for sinners so that no one shall ever again have to go to that prison of fire where people suffer so much."[35] The vision of hell had made quite an

---

[35] John de Marchi, *The Crusade of Fatima: The Lady More Brilliant Than the Sun* (New York: P. J. Kenedy, 1948), 124.

impression on Jacinta, who practiced heroic virtue in such an exemplary way. Her heroic efforts can put even adults to shame. She teaches us to be very generous with God.

The Blessed Mother came down again from heaven to enlighten fragile little Jacinta about what was left of her time on earth. Jacinta would be going to a hospital in Lisbon and would suffer greatly and would not see her family again. Knowing that she would suffer alone was a great pain for her, but by God's grace and her determination, she was able to muster every bit of courage to endure her remaining days alone, since the Blessed Lady had told Jacinta that she would come back to get her and bring her straight to heaven! Can you even imagine this? There would be three more visits from the Blessed Mother to sweet Jacinta.

The youngest visionary would be off to the Lisbon hospital very soon, but not before just one more trip to the Cova da Iria for a few moments of prayer. She had begged her mother to bring her there. Next, she went to say good-bye to her cousin and holy companion Lucia. It was a tear-jerking farewell. The remaining two visionaries hugged one another tightly. Soon Lucia would be left alone to do the work. Jacinta felt compelled to remind Lucia one last time: "You must stay and tell people that God wants to establish in the world devotion to the Immaculate Heart of Mary." She gave her older cousin a little pep talk and some advice: "When you have to say this, don't hide, but tell everybody that God gives us his grace through the Immaculate Heart of Mary and that people must ask it through her and that the Sacred Heart of Jesus wants the Immaculate Heart of Mary by his side. They must ask peace through the Immaculate Heart because God has given it to her."[36]

The Blessed Mother visited Jacinta three times when she was at the Lisbon hospital. She told little Jacinta more about penance and about war being a punishment for sin. She talked about the importance of praying for priests, that some fashions would be designed that would offend God, and more. It was consoling for Jacinta to be in the presence of the Holy Lady because she suffered terribly

---

[36] Marchi, *Fatima: From the Beginning*, 192.

in her last days. She continued to offer all her pain to God. Four days before Jacinta's death, the Blessed Mother came to reassure her that she would be back to get her very soon. On the evening of February 20, 1920, Jacinta was carried to heaven by the Queen of Heaven herself!

HOME TO HEAVEN

Both Francisco and Jacinta had gone home to heaven! When we say that they went *home* to heaven, what do we mean? Heaven is our true home. It is where we are meant to live for all eternity after living out our lives here on earth. When my sister was dying, a Missionary of Charity nun (in Mother Teresa's order) told me something special. She reminded me of Mother Teresa's words about dying. Mother Teresa had said, "Death is nothing except going back to God, where He is and where we belong. Death is the most decisive moment in human life. It is our Coronation: to die in peace with God." These words from my friend the saint give us much to think about.

Our Lady's Message to Three Shepherd Children

On May 13, 2000, both Francisco and Jacinta were beatified by Pope John Paul II. Lucia was present for the solemn Mass of beatification. At that time Lucia was a Carmelite nun and called Sister Maria Lucia.

Pope John Paul II spoke of the brother and sister visionaries in his homily:

What most impressed and entirely absorbed Bl. Francisco was God in that immense light which penetrated the inmost depths of the three children. But God told only Francisco "how sad" he was, as he said. One night his father heard him sobbing and asked him why he was crying; his son answered: "I was thinking of Jesus who is so sad because of the sins that are committed against him". He was motivated by one desire — so expressive of how children think — "to console Jesus and make him happy".

A transformation takes place in his life, one we could call radical: a transformation certainly uncommon for children of his age. He devotes himself to an intense spiritual life, expressed in assiduous and fervent prayer, and attains a true form of mystical union with the Lord. This spurs him to a progressive purification of the spirit through the renunciation of his own pleasures and even of innocent childhood games.

Francisco bore without complaining the great sufferings caused by the illness from which he died. It all seemed to him so little to console Jesus: he died with a smile on his lips. Little Francisco had a great desire to atone for the offences of sinners by striving to be good and by offering his sacrifices and prayers. The life of Jacinta, his younger sister by almost two years, was motivated by these same sentiments.

With regard to little Jacinta, the pontiff said:

Little Jacinta felt and personally experienced Our Lady's anguish, offering herself heroically as a victim for sinners. One day, when she and Francisco had already contracted the illness that forced them to bed, the Virgin Mary came to visit them at home, as the little one recounts: "Our Lady came to see us and said that soon she would come and take Francisco to heaven. And she asked me if I still wanted to convert more sinners. I told her yes". And when the time came for Francisco to leave, the little girl tells him: "Give my greetings to Our Lord and to Our Lady and tell them that I am enduring everything they want for the conversion of sinners". Jacinta had been so deeply moved by the vision of hell during the apparition of 13 July that no mortification or penance seemed too great to save sinners.

She could well exclaim with St Paul: "I rejoice in my sufferings for your sake, and in my flesh I complete what is lacking in Christ's afflictions for the sake of his body, that is, the Church" (Col 1: 24).... And once again I would like to celebrate the Lord's goodness to me when I was saved from death after being gravely wounded on 13 May 1981. I also express my gratitude to Bl. Jacinta for the sacrifices and prayers offered for the Holy Father, whom she saw suffering greatly.[37]

Brother and sister visionaries Francisco and Jacinta had lived exemplary lives of holiness and practiced heroic virtues. You might wonder what exactly heroic virtue or beatification or canonization is? Let's start with heroic virtue. The *Catholic Dictionary* states that heroic virtue is "the performance of extraordinary virtuous actions with readiness and over a period of time. The moral virtues are exercised with ease, while faith, hope, and charity are practiced to an eminent degree." This is what little Francisco and Jacinta showed us. They gave up their own comforts to make reparation for the souls of others. We must pray for the graces to be able to act heroically, and we must also use our free wills to desire to be heroic in virtue.

My friend Servant of God Fr. John Hardon spoke about heroic virtue a lot. He continually encouraged others to practice heroic virtue and said that we live in such a

---

[37] John Paul II, Homily during the beatification of Francisco and Jacinto Marto, May 13, 2000.

darkened, convoluted world that we absolutely need to be heroic in virtue and in faith in order to survive.

I'm reminded also of Servant of God Archbishop Fulton Sheen, who instructed us about the need to be strong in our faith and, in a sense, not to be a "dead body" that will float downstream. He said, "Thirty or forty years ago, it was easy to be a Christian. The very air we breathed was Christian. Bicycles could be left on front lawns; doors could be left unlocked. Suddenly all this has changed; now we have to affirm our faith. We live in a world that challenges us. And many fall away. Dead bodies float downstream; it takes live bodies to resist the current. And this is our summons."[38] He wrote that some time ago, and in many respects our world has become much more challenging. We need to step up to the plate, so to speak, and not be a dead body! We don't want to go with the flow of the culture and float downstream! We must be countercultural.

[38] *Through the Year with Fulton Sheen: Inspirational Selections for Each Day of the Year* (San Francisco: Ignatius Press, 2003), 28.

Now, let's take a quick look at the canonization process since we have just discussed the beatification of the brother and sister visionaries. The Catholic Church beatifies someone to proclaim that person to be holy and on the path to canonization, which is when the person is proclaimed a saint, given to believers as an intercessor and a model of holiness. After much time and examination by the Church, when it is found that the person has lived the Catholic Faith in accordance with his state of life, following God's holy will, and has exhibited heroic virtue, the person is beatified in a special ceremony. Proof of a miracle performed through the help of the holy person is also needed for beatification. The next step is canonization, which requires a second miracle.

Saint John Paul II once noted, "The saints have always been the source and origin of renewal in the most difficult moments in the Church's history."[39] We can certainly look to the saints for inspiration and ask for

[39] John Paul II, Apostolic Exhortation *Christifideles Laici*, December 30, 1988, no. 16.

their helpful intercession. We will talk about the Communion of Saints in the next chapter.

The *Catechism of the Catholic Church* teaches, "By *canonizing* some of the faithful, i.e., by solemnly proclaiming that they practiced heroic virtue and lived in fidelity to God's grace, the Church recognizes the power of the Spirit of holiness within her and sustains the hope of believers by proposing the saints to them as models and intercessors" (CCC 828).

We must not conclude that Francisco and Jacinta were beatified because they saw the Blessed Virgin Mary. No, it was not for that reason that they were raised to the honors of the altar. They could have run away from the visions or could have listened to the Mother of God without carrying out her instructions. Instead, these heroic little children listened attentively, prayed, suffered, and made many sacrifices—trying with all their might to save the souls of sinners and to please our Lord and His holy Mother. We can certainly look to Blessed Francisco and Blessed Jacinta as models of holiness that we can strive to imitate. As well, let's not forget to ask them often for their intercession.

Something to Think About

You have learned that Francisco and Jacinta remained courageous in their faith throughout their lives and even through their last moments. Before the apparitions, they were very obedient and faithful Catholics. As we know, they were chosen by God to live out the message of Fatima, and in doing so they became examples of holiness to the world. Thousands upon thousands of people traveled from all parts of the world to be part of the amazing phenomena. It was three simple shepherd children who listened attentively and followed all of the holy interactions with the Angel of Peace and the Blessed Mother. These three children were examples of heroic virtue not only in their own time, but even now in our time, and they will continue to be so in the future because Our Lady of Fatima's message will continue on.

Can you take a few moments to think about what kind of example you might be to your friends and family? Do you think that your words and actions help others to think about God? If you don't think so, what can you do to change that?

CHAPTER TEN

Lucia's Work Continues

Lucia was now alone. But was she really alone? Wouldn't Francisco and Jacinta be praying along with her from heaven? As Catholics, we believe in something called the Communion of Saints. To understand the Communion of Saints we need to remember that the Catholic Church was founded by Jesus Christ. It includes three levels of existence: the *Church Militant* on earth, the *Church Suffering* in purgatory, and the *Church Triumphant* in heaven. At the end of the world, there will be only the Church Triumphant in heaven.

As Catholics, we believe that we are all connected in this Communion of Saints and that there is communication between the three levels. We on earth can invoke the saints in heaven, asking for their assistance, and we can pray for the souls in purgatory, that they may be relieved of their suffering and get to heaven sooner. Those in heaven pray for the Church Militant on earth and for the relief of the souls in purgatory. Those in purgatory can ask the saints in heaven to help us on earth and can pray for us on earth who are struggling to make it to heaven one day.

Fr. John Hardon describes the Communion of Saints as "the unity and cooperation of the whole Church. Together, we all form one Mystical Body. We share our merits and prayers with one another for the greater glory of God and the upbuilding of Christ's Body which is His Church."[40]

---

[40] Fr. John Hardon, S.J., *The Essentials of the Catholic Faith*, pt. 1, chap. 9, Real Presence Eucharistic Education and Adoration Association, http://www.therealpresence.org/.

HELP FROM HEAVEN

In addition to the help from her little cousins' prayers from heaven, Lucia held tight to the Blessed Mother's promise that she would never forsake her. During the July 1917 apparition, the Holy Mother told Lucia, "Don't lose heart. I will never forsake you. My Immaculate Heart will be your refuge and the way that will lead you to God." Lucia would need to remind herself about the Blessed Mother's promise to her.

Even though there were times when Lucia might have felt a bit overwhelmed at the immensity of the mission entrusted to her by the Blessed Mother, she was very determined to carry out her responsibilities to please the Lord and the Blessed Mother.

As a little girl, Lucia had sometimes thought about becoming a nun. That was on her mind once again, but she first had to learn to read and write, as the Blessed Mother had instructed her. Lucia focused on that goal by getting an education at the local school, where she did well.

IN THE COMPANY OF NUNS

It seemed that everywhere Lucia turned she was bombarded by questions from people about the apparitions of Mary. Lucia was considered a celebrity. She did not want that type of attention. She preferred a quiet contemplative life, but the serene life she knew as a small child had ceased to exist. A new demanding life unfolded. And it wasn't that Lucia didn't want to share with others about the great Mother of God. It was just that answering countless questions and continual requests exhausted her. Some of the people were not very polite when asking, and were sometimes downright demanding.

The new bishop of Leiria, Dom Jose Alves Correia da Silva, knew about the visionary named Lucia dos Santos and was concerned about her being badgered constantly and having no peace and nowhere to hide from the steady bombardment. He arranged for Lucia to be transferred to the Sisters of Saint Dorothy, where she could receive a good and holy education. Lucia entered the college of Dorothean Sisters on June 17, 1921. It was hard to be away from her family, but she put her mind to her studies and her prayers and helped quite a bit with the domestic work as well.

When Lucia was eighteen years old, she entered the Dorothean convent, became a nun, and was known as Sister Lucia. She was thankful for the training that the Dorothean nuns had given her, but she had always dreamed of being a Carmelite. So, in 1948, after receiving special permission from Pope Pius XII, Sister Lucia was transferred to the cloistered Discalced Carmelite Convent in Coimbra, Portugal. In the Carmelite convent, Sister Lucia became known as Sister Maria Lucia of the Immaculate Heart, a name that sounds very fitting, especially because the Blessed Mother had spoken to Lucia about her Immaculate Heart.

The cloistered life would be a change for Lucia. The sisters lead a prayerful life, as others sisters do, but they stay inside the confines of the convent. In her youthful days, Lucia would roam fields and meadows freely with her cousins and flocks of sheep. Now, later in life and until she would depart earth to go to heaven, with the exception of leaving the Carmelite cloister a couple of times when invited by popes to visit the Fatima shrine, she would stay put within the walls of the convent. One of the times Lucia left the convent was on May 13, 2000, for Francisco's and Jacinta's beatification.

LOOKING TO THE CROSS OF JESUS

One might think that to enter a convent is to live in a peaceful environment without any difficulties or challenges. But that is not true. There are always challenges in living with other people and with so many other things as well. There would be adjustments to her new life, but Sister Maria Lucia was very happy finally to embrace the life she was destined to live out at the Carmelite convent. She had quite a few duties. She was very busy with domestic chores, she made rosaries, and she wrote many letters of encouragement to seminarians. She also answered letters from people who sought her prayers and advice.

Sister Maria Lucia remembered well the Angel of Peace's instructions to her and to her two young cousins:

"Make of everything you can a sacrifice, and offer it to God, as an act of reparation for the sins by which He is offended, and in supplication for the conversion of sinners. You will draw down peace upon your country.... Above all, accept and bear with submission, the suffering which the Lord will send you." She would live by these wise, holy words.

When Sister Lucia entered the Carmelite cloister she couldn't help but notice the cross hanging on the wall of her cell. In 1954, Sister Lucia recounted the experience:

When I had the good fortune of entering the Carmelite Order, I was led to the cell, and as I was entering it I fixed my eyes on the big stripped cross that opened its arms to me. Our Reverend Mother Prioress asked me: "Do you know why this cross has no statue [corpus]?" And without giving me time to answer she added: "It is so that you may crucify yourself on it." What a beautiful ideal to be crucified with Christ! That He may inebriate me with gladness of the cross. Here lies the secret of my happiness — not to want or wish for more than to love and suffer for love.[41]

Sister Maria Lucia felt certain that the secret to her happiness was "not to want or wish for more than to love and suffer for love." She would live her life that way, striving always to suffer for love of others. She would do this each day during her daily duties of housekeeping and in her prayers, offering up everything to God and praying to save souls. Any time there was an inconvenience or some sort of suffering, she would immediately give it to God and ask for His graces so that others might be helped. And when she prayed for others, she grew holier. That's what happens when we give our lives to God in holy surrender, as Sister Maria Lucia did. God, in His goodness and love, transforms our souls and makes them more and more like Himself.

Sister Maria Lucia continued on each day, putting one foot in front of the other to walk in faith within

[41] Fox, *The Intimate Life of Sister Lucia*, 313.

her role as a cloistered nun. She was very attentive to the needs around her and strove to become more and more virtuous to please God and help others. She did everything she could to spread the message of Our Lady of Fatima, but she also had to obey her superiors. She couldn't just go ahead and do things out of order or according to her own whims, or even because the Blessed Mother or Jesus wanted something done. Sister Maria Lucia used the word *patience* a lot in the letters she wrote. She knew that a good rule in the spiritual life is to have patience and to pray for patience.

Oftentimes the superiors and directors of religious sisters will give the very humble or seemingly insignificant tasks to the new sisters to help them to remain humble and obedient. For instance, the very best cook might be put in the position of assistant cook so that she can feel humbled and even blessed by being obedient to her superiors. Cleaning toilets and scrubbing floors are other humbling tasks often given to new religious sisters. This reminds me of a story about the time St. Teresa of Calcutta came out of a bathroom at one of the convents and was smiling from ear to ear. One of the sisters asked why she was so happy. She said something like, "One of the sisters here really loves the Lord! That bathroom was sparkling clean!" She meant that that sister wanted to love God as she cleaned the bathroom, which in itself is a humbling task. The saints often teach us that we should do all of our duties out of love for God. We can ask ourselves if that is how we live our lives. It's something we really need to ponder and then put into action.

My point in mentioning the meaning of the humbling or seemingly insignificant work often given to those in religious life is to emphasize an important point. Just because Sister Maria Lucia was chosen by God to receive visits from the Blessed Mother that would ultimately help to change the world did not mean that she would be given special privileges in the convent. An excerpt from a letter that her Mother Superior wrote to the bishop is a very good illustration of Sister Maria Lucia's commitment to doing even the humbling tasks well and also of her shining example of striving for holiness. The superior wrote:

She continues to prepare herself fervently for the religious life, and has had the knack of not, so far, displaying bad behavior to anyone. She continues in her saintly simplicity and humility so much so that she enchants all her companions. I have set her the meanest and humblest duties; no matter what duty I set her, it is always accomplished.[42]

The Mother Superior went on to say that Sister Maria Lucia seemed happy in her role as the kitchen assistant and immediately picked up the slack whenever there was a need. She did not seek to be the highest or the best. She was simply obedient to what was asked of her. We can learn from the Mother Superior that even when given humble tasks, Sister Maria Lucia did them well and with a smile. Her example inspired the others around her. It's important to note that Sister Maria Lucia's life was not easy. She was blessed with visits from Jesus and Mary, but she had many difficulties, sufferings, and illnesses

---

[42] Ibid., 130.

with which to contend. She chose to keep a positive attitude and to offer for the salvation of souls everything she endured. This she did until the end of her life. She died on February 13, 2005, at the age of ninety-seven. Do you remember when the Blessed Mother told little Lucia, "You are to stay here some time longer. Jesus wishes to make use of you to make me known and loved"? That "some time longer" turned out to be a very long time!

Pope John Paul II wrote a letter to Bishop Albino Mamede Cleto of Coimbra the day after Sister Maria Lucia died.

He wrote:

I learned with deep emotion that Sr. Maria Lucia de Jesús of the Immaculate Heart, at the age of 97, has been called by the Heavenly Father to the eternal dwelling place in Heaven. Thus, she has reached the goal to which she always aspired in prayer and in the silence of her convent.

The liturgy of these days has reminded us that death is the common legacy of the sons and daughters of Adam but at the same time assures us that Jesus, with the sacrifice of the Cross, has opened the doors of immortal life to us. Let us remember these certainties of faith at the moment when we say our last farewell to this humble and devout Carmelite who consecrated her life to Christ, Savior of the world.

The visit of the Virgin Mary which Lucia, as a little girl, received at Fatima in 1917 together with her cousins Francisco and Jacinta, was the beginning of a unique mission to which she remained faithful to the end of her days. Sr. Lucia bequeaths to us an example of great fidelity to the Lord and joyous attachment to his divine will.

I recall with emotion my several meetings with her and the bonds of our spiritual friendship that grew stronger with time. I have always felt supported by the daily gift of her prayers, especially during the most difficult moments of trial and suffering. May the Lord reward her abundantly for her great and hidden service to the Church.

I like to think that it was the Blessed Virgin, the same one whom Sr. Lucia saw at Fatima so many years ago, who welcomed her on her pious departure from earth to Heaven. May the Blessed Virgin now accompany the soul of her devout daughter to the beatific encounter with the divine Bridegroom.

I entrust to you, Venerable Brother, the task of conveying the assurance of my spiritual closeness to the Carmelite nuns of Coimbra. For their inner consolation at the time of parting from Sr. Lucia, I impart an affectionate Blessing to them, which I extend to her relatives, to you, to Cardinal Tarcisio Bertone, my special Envoy, and to all those who are taking part in the sacred funeral rite.[43]

We talked about canonizations earlier when we discussed the beatification of Francisco and Jacinta. On April 30, 2008, the cause for canonization opened for Sister

---

[43] John Paul II, Message to the bishop of Coimbra on the death of Sister Lucia, February 14, 2005.

Maria Lucia. At the time of the writing of this book an important part of the canonization process was completed. It took about nine years, from 2008, when Lucia's cause was opened, until this book was written, for all of the testimonies and writings to be gathered and examined.

"Each page that Sister Lucia wrote had to be meticulously analyzed and we are talking of a universe of 10,000 letters that we managed to gather and of a diary with 2,000 pages, in addition to other more personal texts," said Sister Angela Coelho, who is the postulator for the cause of Lucia's canonization, as she was for Francisco and Jacinta.[44]

The postulator, whose role is to oversee the process, explained that Sister Lucia's process took long because she was "a woman who lived almost 98 years, who corresponded with popes, since Pius XII to John Paul II, with cardinals" plus a large number of others.

---

[44] Quoted in Joseph Pronechen, "Sister Lucia of Fatima Takes Step toward Beatification," *National Catholic Register*, February 14, 2017, http://www.ncregister.com/.

Something to Think About

Sister Maria Lucia was often given humble work to do in the convent. She did it happily and strove for perfection. Can you take a few minutes to think about your tasks and chores? Do you do them with joy in your heart? Do you grumble and complain? Can you try hard to be obedient to your parents and those who have authority over you? It will be pleasing to God and will help you to grow in virtue and holiness.

CHAPTER ELEVEN

The Blessed Mother Visits Lucia

While Sister Maria Lucia was a nun in both religious orders, the Blessed Mother came back to visit with her. She gave Lucia very important instructions. We will take a look at them now.

FIRST APPARITION

The Blessed Mother appeared to Sister Lucia when she was a Dorothean nun and requested something called the Communion of Reparation. Sister Lucia's spiritual director asked her to write it down and to write it in the third person. This is what she wrote:

On December 10, 1925, the most holy Virgin appeared to her, and by her side, elevated on a luminous cloud, was [the Christ] Child. The most holy Virgin rested her hand on [Sister Lucia's] shoulder, and as she did so, she showed her a heart encircled in thorns, which she was holding in her other hand. At the same time, the [Christ] Child said: "Have compassion on the Heart of your most holy Mother, covered with thorns, with which ungrateful men pierce it at every moment, and there is no one to make an act of reparation to remove them." Then the most holy Virgin said: "Look, my daughter, at my Heart, surrounded with thorns with which ungrateful men pierce me at every moment by their blasphemies and ingratitude. You at least try to console me and say that I promise to assist at the hour of death, with the graces necessary for salvation, all those who, on the first Saturday of five consecutive months, shall confess [their sins], receive Holy Communion, recite five decades of the rosary, and keeping me company for fifteen minutes while meditating on the fifteen mysteries of the rosary, with the intention of making reparation to me."[45]

The Blessed Mother gave Sister Lucia and the world a great plan to use to make reparation; it is referred to as Communion of Reparation, or the Five First Saturdays devotion. This devotion is to be done on the first Saturday of five consecutive months, and it is to be done with the intention of making reparation to Our Lady for the sins of ingratitude and blasphemy committed against her. Our Lady explained that there are four main parts to it:

1. Go to confession on that Saturday or during the week before or after it.
2. Receive Holy Communion.

---

[45] *Fatima, in Lucia's Own Words,* 195.

3. Recite five decades of the Rosary.

4. Keep our Lady company for fifteen minutes by meditating on the mysteries of the Rosary.

We will discuss the Blessed Mother's requests in this apparition and the Five First Saturdays devotion further a little later on when we talk about the Blessed Mother's peace plan.

SECOND APPARITION

On February 15, 1926, a couple of months after the Blessed Mother appeared to Sister Lucia, a most interesting thing happened. Sister Lucia had a special encounter with a child near the vegetable garden at the convent. She was surprised to see him there, but even more surprised to find out who he was! This is how Sister Lucia described the scene:

On the 15th (of February 1926), I was very busy at my work, and was not thinking of [the devotion] at all. I went to throw out a pan full of rubbish beyond the vegetable garden, in the same place where, some months earlier, I had met a child. I had asked him if he knew the Hail Mary, and he said he did, whereupon I requested him to say it so I could hear him. But, as he made no attempt to say it himself, I said it with him three times over, at the end of which I asked him to say it alone. But as he remained silent and was unable to say the Hail Mary alone, I asked him if he knew where the Church of Santa Maria was, to which he replied that he did. I had him go there every day to say this [prayer]: "O, my heavenly Mother, give me your Child Jesus!" I taught him this, and then left him…. Going there as usual, I found a child who seemed to me to be the same one whom I had previously met, so I questioned him: "Did you ask our heavenly Mother for the Child Jesus?" The child turned to me and said: "And have you spread through the world what our heavenly Mother requested of you?" With that, he was transformed into the resplendent

Child. Knowing then that it was Jesus, I said: "My Jesus, you know very well what my confessor said to me in the letter I read to You. He told me that it was necessary for this vision to be repeated, for further happenings to prove its credibility, and he added that Mother Superior, on her own, could do nothing to propagate this devotion."[46]

Sister Lucia was speaking with the Christ Child! He appeared to her in the form of a little child and then revealed Himself during their conversation. Sister Lucia was in a tight spot with regard to spreading the Blessed Mother's messages to the world. She was living with the vow of obedience as a cloistered nun, and her spiritual director was not yet ready to spread the message of the Five First Saturdays devotion because he wanted more proof that it was necessary. He felt that it wasn't necessary to promote because some people already prayed the Rosary on first Saturdays. The Christ Child told Sister

[46] Ibid, 196–197.

Lucia that many people start a devotion to pray the Rosary on first Saturdays but don't finish.

Sister Lucia would try to do her best to promote the message of the Blessed Mother. She had to listen to her spiritual director and the Mother Superior. She also needed to keep busy with her tasks as a nun and of striving for perfection in the religious life to please our Lord.

THIRD APPARITION

Not quite two years after seeing the Christ Child near the garden, Sister Lucia was still trying hard to promote the messages of the Blessed Mother. She wanted to ask Jesus specific questions. She didn't know how she could answer her superiors about the origin of the devotion to the Immaculate Heart of Mary without disclosing the secret Our Lady told her to keep in the utmost confidence. She needed to ask Jesus how much she could talk about. Was she allowed to speak of any of it to her superiors? As she prayed to Jesus in the chapel, she asked Him these questions. She heard Jesus tell her: "My daughter, write what they ask of you. Write also all that the most holy Virgin revealed to you in the Apparition [July 13], in which she spoke of this devotion. As for the remainder of the Secret, continue to keep silence."[47]

Sister Lucia now knew that she could talk about the Five First Saturdays devotion and still keep the Third Secret (or the third part of the secret) confidential.

REVELATION FROM JESUS

Sister Lucia was transferred to another convent in Tuy, Spain. She was still having trouble promoting the devotion of the Five First Saturdays because no one was supporting her in her efforts. Fr. Jose Bernardo Goncalves, S.J., was Sister Lucia's spiritual director. He wanted to know why the devotion is for *five* Saturdays and not some other amount. Sister Lucia wrote a letter to him on June 12, 1930, and described her encounter and conversation with the Lord in the chapel. This is what she wrote:

[47] Ibid., 195.

Remaining in the chapel with our Lord, part of the night of the 29th–30th of that month of May 1930, talking to our Lord about [some of those] questions, I suddenly felt possessed more intimately by the Divine Presence; and if I am not mistaken, the following was revealed to me: "Daughter, the motive is simple. There are five kinds of offenses and blasphemies spoken against the Immaculate Heart of Mary: blasphemies (1) against her Immaculate Conception; (2) against her perpetual virginity; (3) against her divine maternity, refusing at the same time to accept her as the Mother of mankind; (4) by those who try publicly to implant in the hearts of children an indifference, contempt, and even hate for this Immaculate Mother; and (5) for those who insult her directly in her sacred images."[48]

---

[48] World Apostolate of Fatima, *Spiritual Guide for the Salvation of Souls and World Peace* (Washington, NJ: World Apostolate of Fatima, 2008), 128–129.

Sister Lucia was now certain about the specific kinds of offenses against the Immaculate Heart of Mary. Jesus also told Sister Lucia that His Mother was trying to save her children from hell and asked for these acts of reparation.

FOURTH APPARITION

The Blessed Mother appeared to Sister Lucia on June 13, 1929. Sister Lucia was making a Eucharistic Holy Hour with Jesus. While she was praying alone in the chapel that evening, she saw a most amazing vision! She described it this way:

> I had sought and obtained permission of my Superiors and Confessor to make a Holy Hour from eleven o'clock until midnight, every Thursday to Friday night. Being alone one night, I knelt near the altar rails in the middle of the chapel and, prostrate, I prayed the prayers of the Angel. Feeling tired, I then stood up and continued to

pray with my arms in the form of a cross. The only light was that of the sanctuary lamp. Suddenly the whole chapel was illuminated by a supernatural light, and above the altar appeared a cross of light reaching to the ceiling.

In a brighter light, on the upper part of the cross, could be seen the face of a man and his body as far as the waist; Upon his breast was a dove of light; nailed to the cross, the body of another man. A little below the waist, I could see a chalice and a large host suspended in the air, on to which some drops of blood were falling from the face of Jesus Crucified and from a wound in His side. These drops ran down on to the host and fell into the chalice.

Beneath the right arm of the cross, was Our Lady and in her hand was her Immaculate Heart. (It was Our Lady of Fatima with her Immaculate Heart in her left hand, without sword or roses, but with a crown of thorns and flames.) Under the left arm of the cross, large letters, as if of crystal clear water which ran upon the altar, formed these words: "Grace and Mercy." I understood that it was the Mystery of the Holy Trinity which was shown to me, and I received lights about this mystery which I am not permitted to reveal.[49]

Can you even imagine such a magnificent vision? There is much meaning in every part of it. We might consider that the Blessed Mother is always joined to her Son Jesus' sufferings on the Cross. She is shown in the vision with her Sorrowful Heart. Our loving Mother offers her sufferings to our heavenly Father, begging reparation for the sins of the world and for the salvation of souls.

Mary's place in God's plan is always higher than that of any other person. Mary's Immaculate Heart is a central part of the message of Fatima. The Cross of Jesus is central to our Catholic Faith.

[49] *Fatima, in Lucia's Own Words*, 199–200.

THE BLESSED MOTHER SPEAKS ABOUT CONSECRATION

Sister Lucia remained in prayer after seeing this vision. Then the Blessed Mother spoke to her about a very important moment:

> The moment has come in which God asks the Holy Father, in union with all the Bishops of the world, to make the consecration of Russia to my Immaculate Heart, promising to save it by this means. There are so many souls whom the Justice of God condemns for sins committed against me, that I have come to ask reparation: sacrifice yourself for this intention and pray.[50]

The Blessed Mother was working hard so that souls could be saved. We will discuss more about the consecration to Russia as we continue the story of Our Lady of Fatima.

---

[50] Ibid., 200.

Our Lady's Message to Three Shepherd Children

In our final chapter we will take a further look at the messages of Our Lady of Fatima to the three shepherd children and to the whole world.

Something to Think About

Ever since Lucia was a little child, God had special designs on her soul. He helped to guide her through the visits of the Angel of Peace and the Blessed Mother as well as His own visits to her, and He whispered to her soul when she visited Him in the chapel. Lucia had very important work to do, after all. Just because you do not receive holy visits as Lucia did, however, does not mean that you are less important. God loves you very much. He has an important plan for your life too and wants you to visit Him in prayer often.

Can you take a few moments to think about your life? Can you make a commitment to spend more time in prayer? Is it possible for you to visit Jesus in the Blessed Sacrament in the tabernacle? He awaits your visit! Perhaps you and your family can make a visit to Jesus very soon!

CHAPTER TWELVE

The Blessed Mother's Hopeful Peace Plan

Pope Emeritus Benedict XVI gave very succinct, holy advice when he said, "Learn the message of Fatima! Live the message of Fatima! Spread the message of Fatima!" I hope you have been learning the message of Fatima from this book. I hope that you will live the message through your loving prayers and sacrifices and will strive to spread the message of Fatima! Our Lady of Fatima is counting on all of us believers to share her great message of hope. Let us take another look at the messages of the Blessed Mother.

OUR LADY OF FATIMA'S INSTRUCTIONS

What were the Blessed Mother's instructions, and how can we carry them out? Our Lady of Fatima's message has always been about the need for prayer, penance, and conversion, but it is enveloped in immense hope. The Queen of Heaven gives us much hope and encourages us by reassuring us that in the end her Immaculate Heart will triumph. But why did the Blessed Mother come down to earth with these specific messages that she delivered to the three shepherd children? We will take a look at that.

The Church reiterates the Fatima message and says:

Throughout history there have been supernatural apparitions and signs which go to the heart of human events and which, to the surprise of believers and non-believers alike, play their part in the unfolding of history. These manifestations can never contradict the content of faith, and must therefore have their focus in the core of Christ's proclamation: the Father's love which leads men and women to conversion and bestows the grace required to abandon oneself to him with filial devotion. This too is the message of Fatima which, with its urgent call to conversion and penance, draws us to the heart of the Gospel.[51]

Therefore, the Church states that the message of Fatima emphasizes an urgent call to conversion and penance and "draws us to the heart of the Gospel."

CONVERSION

Let's start with conversion. The *Catechism* states, "Conversion touches the past and the future and is nourished

---

[51] CDF, *The Message of Fatima*.

by hope in God's mercy" (CCC 1490). St. Ambrose taught that there are two kinds of conversion: "There are water and tears: the water of Baptism and the tears of repentance."[52] We can consider an act of conversion when we recall Jesus' telling of the parable of the prodigal son. It is the story of a son who squanders his inheritance, commits sin, and then finally comes back home to his father to beg for forgiveness. His father doesn't simply forgive his son for what he has done. He goes far beyond that and joyfully welcomes his repentant son back with open arms, giving him a beautiful robe, a ring, and a lush banquet. The Church teaches, "All these are characteristic of the process of conversion. The beautiful robe, the ring, and the festive banquet are symbols of that new life—pure, worthy, and joyful—of anyone who returns to God and to the bosom of his family, which is the Church. Only the heart of Christ Who knows the depths of his Father's love could reveal to us the abyss of his mercy in so simple and beautiful a way" (CCC 1439).

[52] Ambrose, *ep.* 41, 12: *PL* 16, 1116.

Some might think of conversion as a once-in-a-lifetime event. But conversion is an ongoing process that can occur each and every day as we pray and ask forgiveness for our shortcomings and strive to come closer to God. We should strive to convert our hearts to become like God. Yes! That's right — like God! That might sound impossible, but let us consider the words of St. John the Baptist, who said, "He must increase, but I must decrease" (John 3:30). We must allow God to come into our hearts and transform us — to convert our hearts and souls! St. Gregory of Nyssa said, "The goal of a virtuous life is to become like God."[53] We must work hard at becoming more and more virtuous each day. After all, God created us to become holy! St. Teresa of Calcutta often said, Becoming holy is really a duty. It is our responsibility to become holy. One of the beautiful things about becoming holy is that it radiates out to others and helps them to desire holiness too.

---

[53] Gregory of Nyssa, *De beatitudinibus*, 1: PG 44, 1200D.

Do you remember how the Blessed Mother continually asked the children to pray for sinners and showed them the vision of hell so that they would see the reality of it and then possess the desire to save souls? Well, when you commit yourself to becoming holy, asking for God's graces and praying as much as you can, you set an amazing example for others. They see the radiance of God's love in your soul and want to imitate it. The ones who do not want to imitate it might very well be positively affected by it anyway. God's love is powerful!

PENANCE

Let's talk about penance. The *Catechism* teaches, "Taking up one's cross each day and following Jesus is the surest way of penance" (CCC 1435). We can recall that, in the vision of the flaming sword in the Third Secret, the angel cried out in a loud voice, "Penance, Penance, Penance!" In *Fatima for Today*, Fatima expert Fr. Andrew Apostoli, C.F.R., writes, "The angel's call to penance reminds us that God intervenes in the world when we do penance." He continues, "As we saw in the Pardon Prayer that the Angel of Peace taught the children, the purpose of penance is to help us believe, adore, trust, and love God."[54]

The Blessed Mother urged the shepherd children to make sacrifices and offer penances for sinners. We can do the same. We are all called by God to possess a spirit of penance. Fr. Apostoli writes, "Penance, willingly embraced by us and achieved by the grace of God, is our contribution to God's work of redemption."[55] We should pause for a moment to ponder how truly amazing that is! We actually cooperate and help with God's work of redemption when we offer penances. Let us make sure when we take on penances, however, that we don't mistakenly make imprudent decisions. For instance, severely fasting or fasting for too long can harm our bodies. We should also avoid doing penance without a good and

---

[54] Fr. Andrew Apostoli, C.F.R., *Fatima for Today* (San Francisco: Ignatius Press, 2010), 86, 87.

[55] Ibid., 87.

cheerful attitude. It would be contradictory to make sacrifices for sinners and to be grumpy about it. God loves a cheerful giver (see 2 Cor. 9:7)!

Fr. Apostoli explains, "Sorrow for our sins is one of the most pleasing and effective penances we can offer the Lord, as we see in the psalm King David prayed after his fall into serious sin: 'The sacrifice acceptable to God is a broken spirit; a broken contrite heart, O God, you will not despise' (Psalm 51:19)."[56]

Let us then be sorrowful for our sins and strive not to commit sins. We can go to the sacrament of Confession often to receive many graces to continue on the road to holiness to which we are called.

CONSECRATION TO THE IMMACULATE HEART OF MARY

The consecration of Russia to the Immaculate Heart of Mary was a very important part of Our Lady of Fatima's

[56] Ibid., 115.

message. Remember, the Blessed Mother told Sister Lucia, "The moment has come in which God asks the Holy Father, in union with all the Bishops of the world, to make the consecration of Russia to my Immaculate Heart, promising to save it by this means. There are so many souls whom the Justice of God condemns for sins committed against me, that I have come to ask reparation: sacrifice yourself for this intention and pray."

The Blessed Mother had told Sister Lucia and her two younger cousins that she would return to request the consecration of Russia to her Immaculate Heart. She foretold that another terrible war would break out during Pope Pius XI's pontificate if people did not stop offending God. She also said there would be a great sign in the sky that would appear before the war. In 1938 there was a magnificent, colorful sky like a brilliant aurora borealis that was sighted all over Europe and parts of the United States.

St. John Paul II explained the meaning of the consecration in his homily on the sixty-fifth anniversary of Fatima. He brings us back to the redemptive Cross and

Jesus' gift of His Mother, Mary, to us. I think it's wise to read his words slowly and to meditate upon them:

On the Cross Christ said: "Woman, behold, your son!" With these words he opened in a new way his Mother's heart. A little later, the Roman soldier's spear pierced the side of the Crucified One. That pierced heart became a sign of the redemption achieved through the death of the Lamb of God.

The Immaculate Heart of Mary, opened with the words "Woman, behold, your son!" is spiritually united with the heart of her Son opened by the soldier's spear. Mary's Heart was opened by the same love for man and for the world with which Christ loved man and the world, offering himself for them on the Cross, until the soldier's spear struck that blow.

Consecrating the world to the Immaculate Heart of Mary means drawing near, through the Mother's intercession, to the very Fountain of life that sprang from Golgotha. This Fountain pours forth unceasingly redemption and grace. In it reparation is made continually for the sins of the world. It is a ceaseless source of new life and holiness.

Consecrating the world to the Immaculate Heart of the Mother means returning beneath the Cross of the Son. It means consecrating this world to the pierced Heart of the Savior, bringing it back "to the very source of its Redemption." Redemption is always greater than man's sin and the "sin of the world." The power of the Redemption is infinitely superior to the whole range of evil in man and the world.

The Heart of the Mother is aware of this, more than any other heart in the whole universe, visible and invisible. And so she calls us. She not only calls us to be converted: she calls us to accept her motherly help to return to the source of Redemption.

Consecrating ourselves to Mary means accepting her help to offer ourselves and the whole of mankind to *Him who is Holy*, infinitely Holy; it means accepting her help by having recourse to her motherly Heart, which beneath the Cross was opened to love for every human being, for the whole world in order to offer the world, the individual human being, mankind as a whole, and all the nations to Him who is infinitely Holy. God's holiness showed itself in the redemption of man, of the world, of the whole of mankind, and of the nations: a redemption brought about through the Sacrifice of the Cross. "For their sake I *consecrate myself*," Jesus had said (John 17:19).

By the power of the redemption the world and man *have been consecrated*. They have been consecrated to Him who is infinitely Holy. They have been offered and entrusted to Love itself, merciful Love.

The Mother of Christ calls us, invites us to join with the Church of the living God in the consecration of the world, in this act of confiding by which the world, mankind as a whole, the nations, and each individual person are presented to the Eternal Father with the power of the Redemption won by Christ. They are offered in the Heart of the Redeemer which was pierced on the Cross.[57]

Perhaps you can take some time soon to pray and meditate upon the Blessed Mother standing at the foot of the Cross with St. John. "When Jesus saw his mother, and the disciple whom he loved standing near, he said to his mother, 'Woman, behold, your son!' Then he said to the disciple, 'Behold, your mother!' And from that hour the disciple took her to his own home" (John 19:26–27). Jesus gifted us with His Mother. We should remember that the Blessed Mother is not someone far away and unreachable; on the contrary, she is very near to us and ready to assist us. St. John Paul II pointed out that Mary the Mother of God calls to us. He explained,

---

[57] John Paul II, Homily during the Mass of Our Lady of Fatima, Fatima, Portugal, May 13, 1982.

"She not only calls us to be converted: She calls us to accept her motherly help to return to the source of Redemption."

ST. JOHN PAUL II AND CONSECRATION

The consecration of Russia to the Immaculate Heart of Mary that the Blessed Mother called for would take many years to accomplish. The Third Secret of Fatima was sealed in an envelope and kept at the Secret Archives at Vatican, not to be opened before 1960. Both Pope John XXIII and Pope Paul VI chose not to publish the contents of the Third Secret of Fatima. Pope Pius XII consecrated the world, and later on Russia, to the Immaculate Heart of Mary. Pope John Paul II had a different perspective on publishing the Third Secret of Fatima, and he also consecrated Russia to the Immaculate Heart of Mary. Let us take a look at the drama that occurred in St. Peter's Square on the sixty-fourth anniversary of the first apparition of Our Lady of Fatima.

On May 13, 1981, a burst of gunfire shocked the thousands gathered in St. Peter's Square and nearly killed the Holy Father. Pope John Paul II was shot four times when a professional assassin named Mehmet Ali Agca aimed to kill the pontiff. Pope John Paul II suffered severe blood loss and was at the brink of death when he arrived at Gemelli Hospital. When he regained consciousness, his very first thoughts were on Fatima. He began to read Sister Lucia's *Memoirs* and her letters during his time of recuperation at the hospital. On July 18, the Holy Father asked for the envelope containing the Third Secret of Fatima.

Pope John Paul II was deeply moved upon reading the contents of the envelope because the reality of the "secret" became instantly crystal clear to him. We recall that in the Third Secret of Fatima a bishop in white was described. The pontiff immediately thought that he should consecrate the world to the Immaculate Heart of Mary. He firmly believed that on May 13, 1981, the sixty-fourth anniversary of the first apparition in Fatima, the Blessed Mother guided the bullets that shot him to protect him from death. Providentially, the Third Secret of Fatima was about him, the "Bishop dressed in white." Pope John Paul II recognized himself as the pope (or bishop) who, in the third part of the secret, was killed. Pope John Paul II was not killed, but believes he was miraculously saved by the Queen of Heaven.

St. John Paul II consecrated Russia and the world to the Immaculate Heart of Mary twice—first on May 13, 1982, and later, more effectively, on March 25, 1984, when he made the consecration in union with the bishops of the Church, as the Blessed Mother requested. Sister Lucia later stated that Pope John Paul II's consecration had satisfied the Blessed Mother.

The last part of Pope John Paul II's heartfelt consecration prayer is this:

> Immaculate Heart! Help us to conquer the menace of evil, which so easily takes root in the hearts of the people of today, and whose immeasurable effects already weigh down upon our modern world and seem to block the paths towards the future! ...

Let there be revealed, once more, in the history of the world the infinite saving power of the Redemption: the power of *merciful Love*! May it put a stop to evil! May it transform consciences! May your Immaculate Heart reveal for all the *light of Hope*!"[58]

THE BLESSED MOTHER'S IMMACULATE HEART: HOPE FOR THE FUTURE!

We can recall that the Blessed Mother told the children a way in which to prevent people from going to hell. She said, "To save them, God wishes to establish in the world devotion to my Immaculate Heart. If what I say to you is done, many souls will be saved and there will be peace." It's important to remember that the Blessed Mother said, "*If* what I say is done, many souls will be

---

[58] CDF, *The Message of Fatima.*

saved and there will be peace." We can ask ourselves whether we are doing what she has asked. The Blessed Mother gives us a way to change the future — to prevent souls from going to hell and to help peace to come; we need to follow her instructions and pray and offer penance and sacrifices.

Pope Emeritus Benedict XVI, when he was Cardinal Joseph Ratzinger, explained the meaning of Mary's Immaculate Heart:

> "My Immaculate Heart will triumph." What does this mean? The Heart open to God, purified by contemplation of God, is stronger than guns and weapons of every kind. The *fiat* of Mary, the word of her heart, has changed the history of the world, because it brought the Savior into the world — because, thanks to her *Yes*, God could become man in our world and remains so for all time. The Evil One has power in this world, as we see and experience continually; he has power because our freedom continually

lets itself be led away from God. But since God himself took a human heart and has thus steered human freedom towards what is good, the freedom to choose evil no longer has the last word. From that time forth, the word that prevails is this: "In the world you will have tribulation, but take heart; I have overcome the world" (*Jn* 16:33). The message of Fatima invites us to trust in this promise.[59]

THE FIVE FIRST SATURDAYS DEVOTION

Another very important part of the Blessed Mother's messages and peace plan for the world is the Five First Saturdays devotion, which I talked about in the previous chapter. The Blessed Mother made a huge promise to us! She said, "I promise to help at the hour of death

[59] Ibid.

with the graces needed for salvation, whoever, on the first Saturday of five consecutive months shall confess and receive Holy Communion, recite five decades of the rosary and keep me company for fifteen minutes while meditating on the fifteen mysteries of the rosary."

St. Louis de Montfort, a Marian priest known for his great love for the Queen of Heaven, reminds us of the power of praying the Rosary: "If you say the rosary faithfully unto death, I do assure you that, in spite of the gravity of your sins, 'you will receive a never-fading crown of glory' (1 Peter 5:4)." He was absolutely convinced of Mary's love and help for those who pray the Rosary. He went on to say, "Even if you are on the brink of damnation, even if you have one foot in hell, even if you have sold your soul to the devil as sorcerers do who practice black magic, and even if you are a heretic as obstinate as a devil, sooner or later you will be converted and will amend your life and will save your soul, if—and mark well what I say—if you say the Holy rosary devoutly every day until death for the purpose of knowing the truth and obtaining contrition and pardon for your sins."

St. John Paul II was deeply inspired by the writings of this saint.

THE FIVE OFFENSES AGAINST THE IMMACULATE HEART OF MARY

When we practice the Five First Saturdays devotion, we pray to make up for the terrible sins committed against the Immaculate Heart of Mary, which Jesus enumerated for Sister Lucia. In the previous chapter, we read Sister Lucia's letter to her spiritual director, Fr. Goncalves, explaining that the devotion involves five Saturdays because our Lord mentioned five kinds of offenses against Mary's Immaculate Heart. We can pray and offer sacrifices and commit ourselves to this devotion. Many Fatima experts, including Fr. Apostoli, have remarked that the Five First Saturdays devotion is the most neglected part of the message of Our Lady of Fatima.

Some folks begin the devotion but don't finish it. Yet it is beneficial to our souls and to the souls of others, and the Blessed Mother has asked for it. We should therefore do our part to be faithful to this devotion, not just once, but as many times as we can.

GROWING IN FAITH, HOPE, AND LOVE

With regard to the meaning and purpose of Our Lady of Fatima's message, Pope Emeritus Benedict XVI, when he was Cardinal Ratzinger, recalled an important insight from Sister Lucia in a conversation with him. "Sister Lucia said that it appeared ever more clearly to her that the purpose of all the apparitions was to help people to grow more and more in faith, hope and love—everything else was intended to lead to this."[60]

Eucharistic Adoration

We recall that the Angel of Peace taught the children a deep reverence and love for Jesus in the Eucharist. All three children were impacted by the angel's visits and

[60] Ibid.

deepened their prayer lives. Little Francisco would often visit his "Hidden Jesus" at St. Anthony's church when he spent time alone there with Jesus in the Blessed Sacrament, reserved in the tabernacle. Jesus spoke to Sister Lucia's heart when she adored Him in the Blessed Sacrament. Many graces are granted to those who spend time in prayer visiting Jesus and praying to make reparation.

We recall also the vision that Sister Lucia received when the Blessed Mother appeared to her on June 13, 1929. Sister Lucia was making a Eucharistic Holy Hour to Jesus. Sister Lucia had said, "I could see a chalice and a large host suspended in the air, on to which some drops of blood were falling from the face of Jesus Crucified and from a wound in His side. These drops ran down on to the host and fell into the chalice."

St. Mother Teresa of Calcutta once told me, "Jesus said, 'I looked for one to comfort me, but found none.' Be that one to comfort Him, through your prayers and good works." Therefore, let's be that "one" to comfort Him through our prayers before Him in the Blessed Sacrament!

Growing in holiness and zeal for saving souls

As you learn and live the messages of Our Lady of Fatima, you will certainly grow in holiness and zeal for saving souls. I love what Fr. Andrew Apostoli says in his book *Fatima for Today*: "As we respond to the messages of Our Lady of Fatima we will grow in our love for God and in our zeal for souls, and we will want to spread the word that the mother of our Lord helped us to become better disciples." He continues, "We will be like the Samaritan woman who, after she spoke with Jesus at the well, could not help but tell her friends and neighbors about him."[61]

In his homily at Fatima, St. John Paul II quoted Scripture to underscore the message of Fatima's essential call to conversion and repentance:

> "Repent, and believe in the gospel" (Mark 1:15): these are the first words that the Messiah addressed to humanity. The message of Fatima is, in its basic nucleus, a call to *conversion and*

---

[61] *Fatima for Today*, 231.

repentance, as in the Gospel. This call was uttered at the beginning of the twentieth century, and it was thus addressed particularly to this present century. *The Lady of the message* seems to have read with special insight the "signs of the times," the signs of our time.

Afterword

The saints have been a powerful force throughout the ages. We are blessed to have recourse to them. During the writing of this book, the cause for the canonization of Blessed Francisco and Blessed Jacinta Marto has moved forward when a second miracle had passed an important phase of the process that is necessary for their canonization.

The first miracle attributed to the intercession of Francisco and Jacinta involved Maria Emilia dos Santos, a Portuguese woman whose miraculous cure from osteo-tuberculosis occurred in 1987. This allowed them to be beatified by Pope John Paul II on May 13, 2000, as the youngest non-martyrs to be beatified in the history of the Church.

Seventeen years later, as I write this book, the second miracle required for the canonization of Jacinta and Francisco, concerning a Brazilian child, was approved by Pope Francis, which means that Francisco and Jacinta will be canonized saints!

There is also exciting news with regard to the cause for canonization of Lucia dos Santos, which moved forward when an important part of the canonization process was completed. All of the volumes of testimonies and writings of Sister Lucia had to be gathered and examined. Once approved, Servant of God Sister Lucia could be declared "Venerable."

The canonization process, as we touched upon earlier, always begins with the diocesan bishops, and then the information is sent to the Holy See to examine and determine whether the analysis of the documents is positive. At that point, the "Servant of God" is proclaimed "Venerable." According to the World Apostolate of Fatima USA:

The second stage of the process consists of the analysis of the miracles attributed to the intercession of the "venerable"; if one of the miracles is considered authentic, the "venerable" is proclaimed "blessed." The blessed is proclaimed saint, when after the beatification there is another miracle duly recognized.

The canonization, an act reserved to the Pope, is a confirmation by the Church that a Catholic faithful is worthy of universal public cult (in the case of the blessed, the cult is diocesan) and of being given to the believers as an intercessor and model of holiness.[62]

The Church is extremely thorough in her canonization process, in which it seems that new saints are actually created. It is wise for us to remember, however, that the Church does not create the saints. It is God

---

[62] "Sister Lucia Closer to Beatification," World Apostolate of Fatima, USA, February 1, 2017, https://wafusa.org/.

and the cooperation of the faithful soul that creates a saint—burnished and tried through life's challenges and miracles.

May we all be edified by the lives of three simple shepherd children, Lucia dos Santos and Francisco and Jacinta Marto, who chose to lead exemplary lives of holiness all the way to heaven. Let us, too, seek paths of holiness, inspired by these three. And let us not be slow in seeking their powerful intercession to help us on our own journeys through life, so that by God's amazing grace we may all meet face-to-face one day in the glories of heaven!

In God's Divine Providence this afterword is written on the feast of Blessed Francisco and Jacinta Marto —February 20, 2017.

APPENDIX A

Prayers Associated with the Apparitions at Fatima

ANGEL OF PEACE PRAYERS

The Pardon Prayer

My God, I believe, I adore, I hope, and I love You! I beg pardon for those who do not believe, do not adore, do not hope, and do not love You. (*Pray three times.*)

The Angel's Prayer

Most Holy Trinity, Father, Son, and Holy Spirit, I adore You profoundly, and I offer You the most Precious Body,

Blood, Soul, and Divinity of Jesus Christ, present in all the tabernacles of the world, in reparation for the outrages, sacrileges, and indifference with which He Himself is offended. And through the infinite merits of His Most Sacred Heart, and the Immaculate Heart of Mary, I beg of you the conversion of poor sinners. (*Pray three times.*)

OUR LADY OF FATIMA PRAYERS
The Sacrifice Prayer

O Jesus, it is for love of You, and for the conversion of sinners and in reparation for the sins committed against the Immaculate Heart of Mary!

The Rosary Decade Prayer

O my Jesus, forgive us; save us from the fire of hell; lead all souls to Heaven, especially those who are most in need. (A version of the prayer commonly used in the United States is: O my Jesus, forgive us our sins; save us from the fires of hell. Lead all souls to heaven, especially those in most need of Your mercy.)

The Eucharistic Prayer

O most Holy Trinity, I adore You. My God, my God, I love You in the most Blessed Sacrament.

Daily Prayer of Consecration

I, _____, a faithless sinner, renew and ratify today in thy Heart, O Immaculate Mother, the vows of my Baptism; I renounce forever Satan, his pomps and works; and I give myself entirely to Jesus Christ, the Incarnate Wisdom, to carry my cross after Him all the days of my life, and to be more faithful to Him than I have ever been before.

Queen of the Most Holy Rosary, in the presence of all the heavenly court, I choose thee this day for my Mother and Mistress. I deliver and consecrate to thee, and to thy Immaculate Heart, as thy child and slave of love, my body and soul, my goods, both interior and exterior, and even the value of all my good actions, past, present, and future; leaving to thee the entire and full right of disposing of me, and all that belongs to me, without exception, according to thy good pleasure, for the greater glory of God, in time and in eternity. Amen.

Shorter Daily Renewal of Consecration
Queen of the Most Holy Rosary, I renew my consecration to you and to your Immaculate Heart. Please accept me, my dear Mother, and use me as you wish to accomplish your designs upon the world. I am all yours, my Mother, my Queen, and all that I have is yours. Amen.

Morning Offering
One of the best times to pray is first thing in the morning. Get into the habit of offering yourself to the Lord as soon as you open your eyes to a new day. You can kneel at the side of your bed if you'd like. Here is a prayer I say every morning. I believe that a Morning Offering gets us started out on the right foot, so to speak.

O Jesus, through the Immaculate Heart of Mary, and in union with the holy sacrifice of the Mass being offered throughout the world today, I offer you all of my prayers, works, joys, and sufferings of this day in reparation for the sins committed against the Immaculate Heart of Mary, for my sins and the sins of the whole world. Amen.

Here is another version of the Morning Offering:
O Jesus, through the Immaculate Heart of Mary, I offer
You my prayers, works, joys, and sufferings of this day for
all the intentions of Your Sacred Heart, in union with
the Holy Sacrifice of the Mass throughout the world, in
reparation for my sins, for the intentions of all my relatives and friends, and in particular for the intentions of
the Holy Father. Amen.

"Radiating Christ"

*As you strive to live out the messages of Fatima given to
us by the Queen of Heaven, here is a special prayer to help
you on your journey. It was written by Blessed John Henry
Cardinal Newman and was a favorite of St. Teresa of Calcutta. Mother Teresa and her Sisters prayed it every day after
receiving Holy Communion. We, too, can pray this prayer
and strive to allow Jesus to shine through us to others.*

Dear Jesus, help me to spread Your fragrance
    wherever I go.
Flood my soul with Your spirit and life.

Our Lady's Message to Three Shepherd Children

Penetrate and possess my whole being so utterly, that
    my life may only be a radiance of Yours.

Shine through me, and be so in me that every soul I
    come in contact with may feel Your presence in my
    soul.

Let them look up and see no longer me, but only
    Jesus!

Stay with me and then I shall begin to shine as You
    shine, so to shine as to be a light to others.

The light, O Jesus, will be all from You; none of it will
    be mine.

It will be you, shining on others through me.

Let me thus praise You the way You love best, by shin-
    ing on those around me.

Let me preach You without preaching, not by words
    but by my example, by the catching force of the
    sympathetic influence of what I do,

the evident fullness of the love my heart bears to You.

Amen.

APPENDIX B

Praying the Rosary

The Rosary is closely linked with the message of Our Lady of Fatima. Each time she appeared to the three shepherd children Lucia, Francisco, and Jacinta, in addition to requesting the daily Rosary, she asked that they offer their prayers for peace in the world. "I am the Lady of the Rosary," our Lady said. "Pray the Rosary every day in honor of Our Lady of the Rosary to obtain peace in the world ... for she alone can save it" (July 13, 1917).

Many popes and saints have revered the Rosary. In his Apostolic Letter *Rosarium Virginis Mariae*, St. John Paul II tells us that the Rosary has been around for ages, "has lost none of the freshness," and is simple, yet profound, as well as very fitting for us to pray. The Rosary is "destined to bring forth a harvest of holiness," the pontiff declared.

It's a very good habit to pray all five decades of the Rosary each day. The Blessed Mother asks this of us. In "How to Pray the Rosary," the United States Conference of Catholic Bishops explained the spiritual rhythm of the Rosary: "The repetition in the Rosary is meant to lead one into restful and contemplative prayer related to each Mystery. The gentle repetition of the words helps us to enter into the silence of our hearts, where Christ's spirit dwells."

I encourage folks to pray the daily Rosary even if it is in bits and pieces. We sometimes feel defeated over not accomplishing praying the entire five-decade Rosary at one time. We can begin our Rosary in the morning and build upon it during the day—decade by decade, especially on very busy days. I believe that we can certainly get a full Rosary prayed when we set our minds and hearts to it.

St. John Paul II pointed out the importance of taking the time to pray the Rosary in a contemplative fashion—at "a lingering pace." He encourages us not to speed through our prayers (*Rosarium Virginis Mariae* 12).

Let's be sure to ponder each mystery (we will discuss the mysteries soon) of each decade of the Rosary at a "lingering pace." If you have not yet gotten into the habit of praying the Rosary daily, don't be afraid to start out with just one decade, meditating as you recite the prayers of the Rosary. Let's now take a look at what the Rosary entails.

THE MYSTERIES OF THE ROSARY

There are four sets of mysteries commemorating the life of Christ that are meditated upon each day of the week. They are as follows:

- *The Glorious Mysteries*: Sundays and Wednesdays, outside of Lent and Advent
- *The Joyful Mysteries*: Mondays and Saturdays, and Sundays during Advent
- *The Sorrowful Mysteries*: Tuesdays and Fridays, and Sundays during Lent
- *The Mysteries of Light*: Thursdays

Our Lady's Message to Three Shepherd Children

The Joyful Mysteries: (1) The Annunciation of the Angel to Our Lady (Luke 1:26–38), (2) The Visitation of Our Lady to Saint Elizabeth (Luke 1:39–56); (3) The Birth of Jesus (Luke 2:1–20); (4) The Presentation of the Child Jesus in the Temple (Luke 2:22–38); (5) The Finding of the Child Jesus in the Temple (Luke 2:41–50).

The Mysteries of Light: (1) The Baptism of Jesus (Matt. 3:13–17), (2) The Wedding at Cana (John 2:1–11) (3) The Proclamation of God's Kingdom and the Call to Conversion (Mark 1:14–15), (4) The Transfiguration of the Lord (Luke 9:28–36), (5) The Institution of the Eucharist (Luke 22:14–20).

The Sorrowful Mysteries: (1) The Agony of Jesus in the Garden (Matt. 26:36–46), (2) The Scourging of Jesus (Matt. 27:24–26), (3) The Crowning with Thorns (Matt. 27:27–31), (4) Jesus' Carrying of the Cross (Luke 23:26–32), (5) The Crucifixion of Jesus (John19:17–30).

The Glorious Mysteries: (1) The Resurrection of Jesus (Matt. 28:1–10), (2) The Ascension of Jesus into

Heaven (Acts 1:6–11), (3) The Descent of the Holy
Spirit on Our Lady and the Apostles (Acts 1:12–14; 2:1–
4), (4) The Assumption of Our Lady (Luke 1:48–49),
(5) The Coronation of Our Lady as Queen of Heaven
and Earth (Revelation 12:1–17).

HOW TO PRAY THE ROSARY

*Begin by holding the rosary beads in your hands, and kiss the
crucifix with devotion. Make the Sign of the Cross.*

In the name of the Father, and of the Son, and of
the Holy Spirit. Amen.

Then, holding the crucifix, pray the Apostles' Creed.

I believe in God, the Father Almighty, Creator
of heaven and earth; and in Jesus Christ, His
only Son, our Lord, who was conceived by the
Holy Spirit, born of the Virgin Mary, suffered
under Pontius Pilate, was crucified, died, and was
buried. He descended into hell; on the third day

He rose again from the dead; He ascended into heaven, and is seated at the right hand of God, the Father almighty; from there He shall come to judge the living and the dead. I believe in the Holy Spirit, the holy Catholic Church, the communion of saints, the forgiveness of sins, the resurrection of the body, and life everlasting. Amen.

On the first large bead, pray an Our Father.

Our Father, Who art in heaven, Hallowed be Thy Name; Thy Kingdom come; Thy Will be done on earth as it is in Heaven. Give us this day our daily bread; and forgive us our trespasses as we forgive those who trespass against us; and lead us not into temptation, but deliver us from evil. Amen.

On next three beads, pray three Hail Marys and ask for an increase in the virtues of faith, hope, and charity. Conclude with a Glory Be.

Hail Mary, full of grace, the Lord is with thee; blessed art thou among women, and blessed is the fruit of thy womb, Jesus. Holy Mary, Mother of God, pray for us sinners, now and at the hour of our death. Amen.

Glory be to the Father, and to the Son, and to the Holy Spirit. As it was in the beginning, is now, and ever shall be, world without end. Amen.

For each of the five decades, on the large bead (or medallion) announce the mystery. You may read a brief passage from Scripture, if you desire (see the passages listed earlier with the mysteries). Then pray an Our Father.

On each of the ten smaller beads of each decade, pray a Hail Mary while meditating on the mystery for that decade. Then pray a Glory Be.

After finishing each decade, you may add the Fatima Prayer, which was requested by the Blessed Virgin Mary at Fatima.

O my Jesus, forgive us our sins; save us from the fires of hell; lead all souls to Heaven, especially those who have most need of Thy mercy.

Our Lady's Message to Three Shepherd Children

After the five decades, pray the Hail, Holy Queen.

Hail, holy Queen, mother of mercy, our life, our sweetness, and our hope. To thee do we cry, poor banished children of Eve. To thee do we send up our sighs, mourning and weeping in this valley of tears. Turn then, most gracious advocate, thine eyes of mercy toward us, and after this our exile, show us the blessed fruit of thy womb, Jesus. O clement, O loving, O sweet Virgin Mary.

Leader. Pray for us, O Holy Mother of God.

Response. That we may be made worthy of the promises of Christ.

Leader. Let us pray:

Response. O God, whose only-begotten Son, by His life, death, and Resurrection, has purchased for us the rewards of eternal life, grant, we beseech thee, that while meditating on these mysteries of the most holy Rosary of the Blessed Virgin Mary, we may imitate what they contain and obtain what they promise, through the same Christ our Lord. Amen.

If you desire, you can say the following:

Most Sacred Heart of Jesus, have mercy on us.
Immaculate Heart of Mary, pray for us.

Conclude the Rosary with the Sign of the Cross.

A POWERFUL SACRAMENTAL

A rosary is not merely a string of beads—when blessed, it is a magnificent and powerful sacramental of our Church. St. Padre Pio called it a "weapon" for our times. You will recall that the Blessed Mother showed Lucia, Francisco, and Jacinta the vision of hell, where sinners go because there is no one to pray for them. Knowing this, we should be encouraged to pray many Rosaries for sinners. We can also feel renewed and strengthened in our prayer lives, aware that many saints have also prayed the daily Rosary. Mother Mary never fails to help those who pray her Rosary, and she forever pushes us forth toward her Son Jesus.

It was Sister Lucia herself who reminded us, "The Most Holy Virgin in these last times in which we live has given a new efficacy to the recitation of the Rosary to such an extent that there is no problem, no matter how difficult it is, whether temporal or above all spiritual, in the personal life of each one of us, of our families . . . that cannot be solved by the Rosary. There is no problem, I tell you, no matter how difficult it is, that we cannot resolve by the prayer of the Holy Rosary." Let us heed Lucia's words.

Finally, dear reader, do your best to pray the daily Rosary and encourage others to do so as well, especially your family members. Pope Pius XI tells us that our Rosaries will "put the demons to flight" and will "keep [us] from sin." Holding your rosary beads can comfort you and remind you of Mother Mary's help and her presence when you feel frightened, confused, or concerned.

Keep your blessed rosary with you as a special holy protection and a constant reminder of the Blessed Mother in your life, as well as a reminder of the powerful prayers that she would like you to pray.

May God continue to bless you, and may Mother Mary keep you close to her Immaculate Heart!

Acknowledgments

With a grateful heart to all who have guided me, prayed for me, and loved me throughout my life: my family and friends, especially my parents, Eugene Joseph and Alexandra Mary Cooper, and my brothers and sisters, Alice Jean, Gene, Gary, Barbara, Tim, Michael, and David—I am eternally indebted. With that said, I should also thank those who did harm to me in some way, because by God's grace, they have helped to shape my life as well.

My children have always been my utmost vocation. I love you, Justin, Chaldea, Jessica, Joseph, and Mary-Catherine! My grandson, Shepherd James—I love you, too! My husband, Dave, the wind beneath my wings, thank you for your love and support!

I owe a special thanks to Fr. Andrew Apostoli, C.F.R., for his friendship, his prayers, and his heartfelt letter to parents and caregivers that graces the beginning of this book. His great work on Our Lady of Fatima is a marvelous aid to our spiritual journeys! And to my dear "Sisters in Christ" for their many prayers that continually help to sustain me in my work and ministry. I am also grateful for the intercession of three of my dear saint friends in heaven: Fr. John A. Hardon, S.J., Fr. Bill C. Smith, and St. Teresa of Calcutta (in my heart she remains Mother Teresa).

Heartfelt thanks to Charlie McKinney and the wonderful team at Sophia Institute Press for their partnership in getting this book out to you. Loving prayers for all who are connected through my books, talks, and pilgrimages — thank you for joining me in prayer on the spectacular journey that leads to eternal life. And, of course, I also thank my guardian angel, my wonderful personal assistant.

About the Author

Donna-Marie Cooper O'Boyle is a Catholic wife, mother, grandmother, pilgrimage host, extraordinary minister of the Eucharist, and bestselling and award-winning author of more than twenty books, including: *The Miraculous Medal: Stories, Prayers, and Devotions*; *Feeding Your Family's Soul: Dinner Table Spirituality*; *The Domestic Church: Room by Room*; *Prayerfully Expecting: A Nine-Month Novena for Mothers to Be* (foreword by Mother Teresa); *Embracing Motherhood*; *Rooted in Love: Our Calling as Catholic Women*; *Catholic Mom's Café: 5-Minute Retreats for Every Day of the Year*; *Mother Teresa and Me: Ten Years of Friendship*; *Angels for Kids*; *A Catholic Woman's Book of Prayers*; and *Our Lady of Fatima: 100*

Years of Stories, Prayers, and Devotions. She is also an award-winning journalist, speaker, catechist, and retreat leader. She is the EWTN television host and creator of Everyday Blessings for Catholic Moms, Catholic Moms Café, and Feeding Your Family's Soul.

Donna-Marie enjoyed a decade-long friendship with St. Teresa of Calcutta and received spiritual direction from Servant of God John A. Hardon, S.J. She has received apostolic blessings from St. John Paul II and Pope Emeritus Benedict XVI as well as a special blessing from St. John Paul II on her writing on Mother Teresa.

Donna-Marie is a frequent guest on national television and radio. In 2009 she was listed as one of the "Top Ten Most Fascinating Catholics" in *Faith and Family Live.* Her memoir is entitled *The Kiss of Jesus: How Mother Teresa and the Saints Helped Me to Discover the Beauty of the Cross.*

Learn more about Donna-Marie and her ministry and pilgrimages at www.donnacooperoboyle.com and www.feedingyourfamilyssoul.com.

About the Illustrator

Ann Kissane Engelhart is an accomplished watercolor artist, illustrator, and educator. *Our Lady's Message to Three Shepherd Children and the World* is her seventh illustrated book. She has worked with Amy Welborn to produce the children's books *Friendship with Jesus*, *Be Saints!*, *Bambinelli Sunday*, and *Adventures in Assisi*. She also collaborated with Nancy Brown and Regina Doman on *The Chestertons and the Golden Key*. Her portraits, still-life, and landscape paintings are featured in galleries and private collections. She lives in New York with her husband and children.

Sophia Institute

Sophia Institute is a nonprofit institution that seeks to nurture the spiritual, moral, and cultural life of souls and to spread the Gospel of Christ in conformity with the authentic teachings of the Roman Catholic Church.

Sophia Institute Press fulfills this mission by offering translations, reprints, and new publications that afford readers a rich source of the enduring wisdom of mankind.

Sophia Institute also operates two popular online Catholic resources: CrisisMagazine.com and CatholicExchange.com.

Crisis Magazine provides insightful cultural analysis that arms readers with the arguments necessary for navigating the ideological and theological minefields of the day. Catholic Exchange provides world news from a Catholic perspective as well as daily devotionals and articles that will help you to grow in holiness and live a life consistent with the teachings of the Church.

In 2013, Sophia Institute launched Sophia Institute for Teachers to renew and rebuild Catholic culture through service to Catholic education. With the goal of nurturing the spiritual, moral, and cultural life of souls, and an abiding respect for the role and work of teachers, we strive to provide materials and programs that are at once enlightening to the mind and ennobling to the heart; faithful and complete, as well as useful and practical.

Sophia Institute gratefully recognizes the Solidarity Association for preserving and encouraging the growth of our apostolate over the course of many years. Without their generous and timely support, this book would not be in your hands.

www.SophiaInstitute.com
www.CatholicExchange.com
www.CrisisMagazine.com
www.SophiaInstituteforTeachers.org